'Bought 2 Horses & a Wagon'

'Bought 2 Horses & a Wagon'

The Story of the Murphy Companies
1904–2004

VIRGINIA BRAINARD KUNZ

Foreword by
MARY LETHERT WINGERD

RAMSEY COUNTY HISTORICAL SOCIETY
St. Paul, Minnesota

Production Credits

Research Assistant: Jane Angrist
Text Design: Will Powers, Will Powers Typography
Dust Jacket Design: Lois Stanfield,
    LightSource Images
Endsheets Design: Lu Patterson, Murphy
    Warehouse Company, and Lois Stanfield,
    LightSource Images
Composition: Stanton Publication Services
Printing and Binding: Sexton Printing
Indexing: John M. Lindley, John M. Lindley &
    Associates
Production Management: John M. Lindley,
    John M. Lindley & Associates

Unless otherwise noted, all photographs are from the Murphy Warehouse archives.

Richard T. Murphy Sr. (left) and Edward L. Murphy Jr.

We dedicate this book to Edward L. Murphy Jr. and Richard T. Murphy Sr.
Their strong work ethic, excellent business acumen, and forward thinking
have given our family the blessings we enjoy today.
We hope that future generations of the Murphy Family will also measure up
to the high level of excellence that you have both established.

With loving gratitude,
the Fourth Generation.

Contents

Foreword

FOR MOST OF THE TWENTIETH CENTURY, the Murphy logo
was as much a part of the landscape of St. Paul, Minnesota as
the cathedral at the apex of Summit Avenue or the glowing
number one atop the First National Bank Building. In some ways, the
fleet of distinctive Murphy trucks was even more emblematic of the
city than its stationary monuments. After all, St. Paul grew and flourished as a transportation hub and for generations the movement and
storage of goods constituted the lifeblood of its economy. Yet, before
the publication of this volume, probably few if any St. Paulites knew
or could imagine what a compelling part of the city's history lay behind those familiar trucks. The story of the Murphy Companies is a
many-layered drama—a dynamic story of family struggle, loyalty,
heartache, and achievement; a quintessential tale of Irish networking
and political savvy grounded in the particular social relations of St.
Paul; and a story of national significance as well, one that vividly illu-
minates the impact of state and federal policy on the fortunes of entrepreneurs, workers, and entire industries.

The first Edward Murphy, son of Irish immigrants and founder of
what was to become a family trucking dynasty, was fortunate to be
born in the right place at the right time. In the mid-nineteenth century, when discrimination against the Irish was rampant throughout
most of the United States, the small town of St. Paul was a notable ex-
ception to prevailing prejudices—already well on its way to becoming
a stronghold of Irish influence and social status. One contemporary
described the city as simply "a heaven for the Irish." In 1863, the year
of Murphy's birth, Minnesota's capital also was entering a prolonged
era of explosive growth as it transformed itself from frontier outpost
to urban entrêpot. In this bustling economy, the early establishment
of the Catholic Church and dominant influence of the Democratic
Party had created exceptional avenues of opportunity for Irish up-
and-comers—and E. L. Murphy made the most of them.

Nurtured by a powerful ethnic support system, Murphy developed into a consummate St. Paul-style Irish politician. What that required in a city where the Irish were not dominant in numbers was a talent to reach out across ethnic differences to maintain a Democratic majority and, at the same time, make the most of the ties of Irish brotherhood. As a saloonkeeper in the city's multiethnic North End, Murphy apparently proved a master at the craft. In the nineteenth century, working-class saloons functioned as far more than a recreational space. They were centrally important neighborhood institutions for immigrant workers. They served as a bank for cashing paychecks, a social center, an informal employment agency, a political hub, and provided a free lunch to top it off. Successful saloonkeepers often evolved into popular politicians and delivered working-class votes for the Democratic Party. Murphy must have excelled in this role. He became a confidante of the city's most influential Democratic power broker and in 1894, ten years after opening his first saloon, he was elected alderman from the rough and tumble North End.

E. L.'s brother, Jack, also profited from the web of ethnic and political connections. When the Irish Butler brothers won the contract to build the new state Capitol, the biggest construction project to be undertaken by the young state, they spread the wealth generously among fellow Irish Democrats. Jack Murphy parlayed a team of horses and a wagon into a good living, hauling materials for the project. When the Capitol was completed in 1904, Jack apparently looked for a less strenuous occupation and found a home in the St. Paul police force—no doubt aided by his brother's political clout. E. L., however, must have recognized burgeoning opportunities within the Irish construction and transportation network. He promptly purchased Jack's team and wagon and launched himself into the business of moving goods and materials. Thus, Murphy Transfer entered the roster of successful Irish entrepreneurial ventures that became pillars of St. Paul's economy. That first generation of family-owned businesses created a thick web of mutual assistance that passed business to one another and helped fellow Irish Democrats up the ladder from laborer to the middle class.

E. L. never forgot his roots. Active in politics—either formally or behind the scenes—for most of his life, he regularly used his political and business leverage to secure jobs for Democratic constituents. Despite his increasing wealth, as long as he was active in business and politics he also continued to live in the North End. Quite likely, his working-class sensibilities, and those of his fellow Irish entrepreneurs, influenced the largely harmonious nature of labor relations in

St. Paul. In many ways, he conformed to the classic model of the ethnic success story. In the particular world of St. Paul, his career embodied the particular circumstances and strategies that in just two generations catapulted talented Irish Catholics into the ranks of city social and business leaders.

The evolution of the Murphy Companies also reflects a larger economic and political history—the transformation of the laissez-faire economy of the nineteenth century to the rise and devolution of government regulation in the twentieth. In the teaming business, horses and wagons soon gave way to motorized vehicles and local carriers were able to expand their range of operations. By the 1920s road transportation had begun to compete with rail, creating chaotic competition. In an attempt to stabilize rates, government intervention soon complicated the infant trucking industry. First the state and then the Interstate Commerce Commission imposed regulation on trucking concerns which had previously relied only on personal contacts, usually on a face-to-face basis. Yet, in this transitional era, established personal and political relationships continued to wield significant influence. Thanks to E. L. Murphy's savvy and experience, Murphy Transfer was usually successful in securing the necessary approvals for hauling, which allowed the company to enlarge its scope beyond the city and the state. Regulation proved a boon for both the company and its workers, controling cutthroat competition and also eventually leading to a strengthened position for union labor as well.

Under regulation, three generations of the Murphy family weathered economic downturns and intra-company disputes to build the Murphy Companies into a nationally recognized leader in the transportation industry. Over the years these various Murphy businesses provided thousands of good-paying, union jobs to its employees. Deregulation in the 1980s, however, had a destabilizing effect that regional, unionized firms—no matter how well managed—could not withstand. Seemingly overnight, the familiar Murphy trucks disappeared from the streets and highways. Fortunately, due to farsighted diversification strategies, the company was positioned to shift much of its resources into specialized services and warehousing operations. Securing license as a designated free trade zone, Murphy Warehousing was able to take advantage of the exponential growth in international commerce. Just as earlier generations of the family had adjusted business strategies to changes in technology and market demand, this new direction suggests opportunities for further growth. Still, what remains clear is that today forces beyond local control increasingly drive even family-owned businesses.

At heart, however, the history of the Murphy Companies is fundamentally local, the saga of a family and a community, replete with triumphs and disappointments, joys and sorrows: A story of enormously hard work and innovation; of family loyalty and painful rifts; of sons who learned the business from the bottom up, shouldered the challenges and responsibilities of adversity and made the most of them. It is also the story of a remarkable woman, May McGinnis Murphy, who was a gallant partner—in life and business—in the worst as well as the best of times.

For all its national scope, the Murphy Companies remained rooted in St. Paul, entwined in the lives of generations of friends, business associates, employees, civic partners, and neighbors who helped the company grow. A long family tradition of civic engagement has contributed much to the city in return. Whatever surprising challenges the twenty-first century has in store for this enduring family-owned enterprise, today's generation of Murphys have an admirable legacy to guide them.

Mary Lethert Wingerd

Preface

From "two horses and a wagon" to today's 420-horsepower wagon running inside just one truck, the story you are about to enter is the journey of the Murphy family of St. Paul, Minnesota, as it grew and prospered while surviving many national economic events and defying the statistics of family businesses. It is the family and ecological story of Irish immigrants who started as raw entrepreneurs. Through time and life's lessons, the Murphys' various companies evolved from traditional "family" firms to become professionally operated organizations run by successive generations.

It is also the story of how one family endured early St. Paul politics, the Great Depression, a violent labor uprising in Minneapolis during the 1930s, the post-World War II economic boom, changing technologies and business practices, the trauma following the deregulation of the transportation industry in the 1980s, and the many generational handoffs that a family-owned business may experience.

In a world in which most family businesses last only two generations, I sit today writing this Preface as a member of the fourth generation to run the family enterprises. As a family, we have come to recognize that our history is in many ways one of our most precious assets. I believe the Murphy family has survived because of its core values, which become evident as the story unfolds. These include courage and imagination in taking chances; pride, persistence, and humility during good and bad times; and above all, integrity in every matter. It is a heritage the family treasures immensely and nurtures today as we raise our future generations.

Another core value the family lives by is giving back to our community, which has blessed us in business and allowed us to support the lives of so many other community members as employees, suppliers, customers, and friends. It is in this spirit that I, on behalf of the entire Murphy family, offer our story to you so that others may learn and benefit it from it, or simply enjoy the wild ride unfolding within this book. We look forward to our next 100 years of business and association with our community of friends and neighbors. Warm regards.

Richard T. Murphy Jr.
President
August 10, 2004

Author's Acknowledgments

THE STORY OF THE MURPHY FAMILY and their companies
began, as so many stories do, with the distilling of those accounts that have been embedded in the memories of the
people who lived them. This book began five years ago with a phone
call from Richard T. Murphy Sr., announcing that it was time "to tell
these family stories to a wider audience." Inevitably this account of
one family and their several businesses would, however, be cast against
a more general history of the trucking and warehouse industries in
Minnesota and the nation and that it also would reflect some of St.
Paul's colorful history during the century that lay between 1904 and
2004.

I am therefore deeply indebted to Dick Murphy and his own love
of history, for setting this project in motion. Both he and his brother,
Ed, spent hours with me, as we recorded their memories on tape. It is
said that memories are fleeting, but it was not so for these men. They
spoke with precision and candor in recalling those eventful years.
Both have also honored the cause of history by preserving the remarkable company archives that I was able to draw upon intensively.

No book is the product of one person. I am doubly indebted to
Laurie Murphy, who carefully guided and monitored this project
since its inception, and to her brother, Richard T. Murphy Jr., for his
support and for contributing the Preface to this book. Other family
members searched their memories for me in recounting the years
they grew up in the family and the Murphy Companies: Carole Murphy Faricy, Patricia Murphy Millard, Peter Maas, Edward L. (Mike)
Murphy III and his brothers, Brian and Kevin. I also thank Will Powers for his elegant design of the book; Lois Stanfield for producing a
beautiful jacket for the book; Wendy Holdman at Stanton Publications for translating Will's design into type; and Mike Poquette at Sexton Printing, whose professionalism brought it all together.

Pat Sullivan, John Solum, Mike Butchert, Paul Welna, Ron Gunderson, and Doug Horn all shared their recollections of their years

with the Murphy Companies. Many of the photographs in this book were the work of Mary Boudreau. Others came from Susan Lightfoot. As a researcher, Jane Angrist helped me wade through the mass of invaluable documents in the company archives

This project, however, would not have been possible without the steady guidance of John M. Lindley, an independent researcher and writer and a noted historian in his own right. It was he who undertook the complicated production process that moved my manuscript from type to the book you see today. Finally, and most importantly, I thank Mary Lethert Wingerd, author of the fascinating history, *Claiming the City – Politics, Faith, and the Power of Place in St. Paul* for contributing a gracious and insightful Foreword to this volume.

Virginia Brainard Kunz

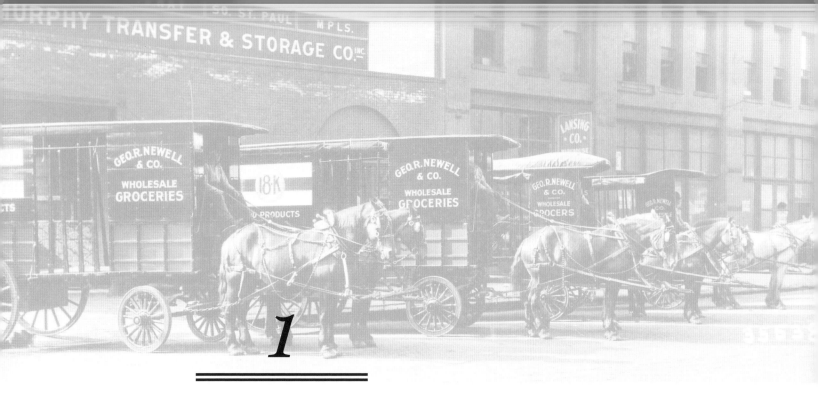

1

'Bought 2 Horses & Wagon from Jack Murphy'

SOMETIME IN 1904, a St. Paul saloonkeeper turned politician bought a team of horses and a wagon and launched a company that would grow into a multimillion dollar enterprise and provide heady financial success, as well as some personal anguish.

Edward L. Murphy Sr., the first of his family to bear that name, would become a community leader as a St. Paul alderman, a Public Works commissioner, and founder of today's Murphy Companies. Along the way, he would ally himself with a major figure in Minnesota's Democratic politics.

Murphy was born into the city's fledgling Irish community on April 15, 1863, and baptised a year later on April 4, 1864, in the old Catholic Cathedral in downtown St. Paul. Or so the records suggest, but they vary, sometimes widely. In a young community where records of births, baptisms, and deaths were kept so casually that they often failed to survive the pioneer period, some confusion surrounds the early years of both Edward Murphy and his brother, John. Apparently the only other child in this Irish Catholic family, John, known as Jack, was a St. Paul policeman who also played a role in the founding of the Murphy Companies. Police department records list his birth date as 1867, as 1873, a date then crossed out and changed back to 1867—not surprising for a police department where more than one John Murphy might well have been serving at that time. However, his

St. Paul in 1857, its domed and pillared territorial capitol at Tenth and Wabasha showing prominently. The St. Paul City Directory for 1856-57 lists a John Murphy as living on Robert "above 6th," a home that would have been among the huddle of houses to the far right. From photographer B. F. Upton's panorama shot from the roof of the first Ramsey County courthouse. Minnesota Historical Society collections.

death certificate lists his birth date as September 19, 1860, and the archives of the Archdiocese of Minneapolis and St. Paul record the baptism of a John Murphy on October 16, 1860, a rite performed by Father Louis Caillet, who entered St. Paul history earlier that year when he accompanied Annie Bilansky to the scaffold after her conviction for murdering her husband.

Then there is the mystery surrounding the Murphy brothers' parents. According to the information available, both were born in Ireland. In the 1900 census, Edward Murphy listed his father's name as John Murphy and Ireland as his place of birth. In Edward Murphy's own death certificate and that of his brother, John, their father also is listed as John and his place of birth as Ireland. Edward Murphy's

St. Paul's third Cathedral, between Wabasha and St. Peter on Sixth Street, around 1860. The two Murphy sons were baptised here in the early 1860s. On the right is the Bishop's residence and behind it is the second Cathedral fronting on Wabasha. St. Paul's first Cathedral was the little chapel Father Lucien Galtier built in 1841 on the bluff above the Mississippi. Photo by R. W. Ransom, Minnesota Historical Society collections.

grandson remembers that his grandfather once said, "All the Murphys came from County Cork." The well-known Murphys of Cork have been brewing their famous Irish stout since 1850, but any direct relationship between St. Paul's John Murphy and possible kinsmen in Cork is unknown. No family stories or records tracing John Murphy's emigration to America—its date, the ship that carried him, his port of entry—not even stories of his earliest years in this country have passed down through the generations. The baptismal records of his sons even confuse his name, inexplicably listing him as Edward, not John. They agree only on the name of their mother. She was Mary O'Brien.

Unknown, too, is when John and Mary O'Brien Murphy were born. While the 1900 census did not list John Murphy's birth date, both parents very likely were born around 1840. There is no record, however, and no family stories of when or where they were married, and when they arrived in St. Paul. Perhaps they were among those who fled the devastating potato famine that began its sweep through Ireland in 1845, but their names do not appear among the residents of St. Paul in 1850, when more than sixty settlers identified Ireland as their place of birth.

However, the *St. Paul City Directory for 1856–57* lists a John Murphy, laborer, living on Robert Street "above 6th" in downtown St. Paul. Edward Murphy once told the *St. Paul Globe* that he was born on the site of the Golden Rule Department Store at Robert and Eighth Street, a location that fits the description of "above 6th."

What *is* known is that John and Mary Murphy were in St. Paul by 1860 when their son John was christened at the Cathedral. If they were living "above 6th" by the mid-1850s, they were in St. Paul at a boom time in the city's history when jobs for laborers like Murphy were plentiful. The community's population had exploded from 910 in 1849, when Minnesota became a territory, to more than 4,000 in 1854, when St. Paul received its charter as a city; three years later, its population was close to 10,000. Murphy's fellow Irish immigrants had organized early in St. Paul. The first St. Patrick's Day celebration was held in 1851. The Benevolent Society of the Sons of Erin was founded in the mid-1850s. A Catholic Temperance Society was established by Bishop

Steamers "Diamond Jo" and "Canada" at the busy Jackson Street landing in St. Paul around 1860, the year the first of the Murphy brothers was baptized. For the young Murphy family, this would have been a daily scene during the shipping season. Minnesota Historical Society photograph.

Joseph Cretin in 1852. Ethnic and religious connections were important. Murphy's fellow countrymen gravitated toward the security and status of government jobs where well-positioned friends found places for them on the police force or on city-sponsored construction projects.

With new arrivals pouring into St. Paul, building was proceeding at a furious pace and lumber was becoming so scarce that some of the newcomers had to sleep on the steamboats that brought them. Parts of the frontier community looked as though an earthquake had struck. Blasting and grading for streets that were being cut through the rocky terrain left behind yawning ditches and huge piles of rubble.

Ox Carts on Third Street

The territorial Capitol, a pillared Greek temple, was completed in 1851 on a square bounded by Tenth, Exchange, Wabasha, and St. Peter Streets, not far from the house on Robert "above 6th" where Edward Murphy would be born. Nearby, a little waterfall tumbled over a ledge at what is now Tenth and Cedar, its stream flowing through a deep ravine between Jackson and Sibley. Lowertown was even then St. Paul's warehousing, trading, and transportation center because it was close to the steamboat landing at the foot of Jackson Street. John Murphy very likely would have seen the hundreds of Red River ox carts that screeched their way down Third Street during the summer months and the many steamboats that tied up at the landing each season.

St. Paul, like most frontier settlements, was known as a "fast" town with the common problems of drunkenness, violence, prostitution, and disorderly conduct. "Gamblers, conmen, thieves, and prostitutes thronged the hotels and streets," historian J. Fletcher Williams wrote in his *History of the City of Saint Paul to 1875*. Speculators in land poured off steamboats daily and, equipped with nothing more than town-site maps and packets of blank deeds, set up shop on the city's sidewalks.

As delegates to the state Constitutional Convention toiled away in Stillwater to prepare Minnesota Territory for statehood, back in St. Paul Joe Rolette, fur trader and territorial legislator, saved the state capital for St. Paul by the simple expedient of stealing the bill that would have moved it to St. Peter. Tucking

ST. PAUL IN THE SUMMER OF 1856:

"Sometimes eight or ten boats would be in port at once, each with large crews of low ruffians who would roam about the city maddened with liquor, and committing excesses, and the small police force (four men) were able to do but little. A public meeting was held, at which a secret police, or sort of vigilance committee, was appointed to aid the authorities."

J. FLETCHER WILLIAMS *in* The History of the City of Saint Paul to 1875.

it into his pocket, he strolled over to Truman and Smith's bank in the Fuller House at Seventh and Jackson, a block from the Murphy home, locked the bill in the vault and hid out until the deadline for signing it into law had passed.

* * *

John Murphy had put down his roots in a vibrant community, but its exuberance dimmed as the real estate mania that drove the prosperity of the 1850s dissolved in the Panic of 1857. It was set off in August by the failure of the Ohio Life Insurance and Trust Company in New York to collect on its heavy loans against railroad stock. When the company suspended, the ripples were

One of Norman Kittson's Red River Ox Carts and its driver on Third Street (now Kellogg Boulevard) around 1858–1859. The squeal emitted by the carts' ungreased axles would have been a familiar summer sound for the Murphy family on Robert "above 6th." Photo by James E. Martin, Minnesota Historical Society collections.

felt even in far-off St. Paul. Money promptly dried up. So did the construction work that was the lifeblood of laborers like Murphy. Five hundred men had been at work all that summer grading the downtown streets and 343 buildings had gone up that season. Gaslights would illuminate Third Street by fall.

In the winter of 1857, Ramsey County began to issue scrip in lieu of cash. Currency no longer was available to lend, even at four or five percent a month; men like Henry McKenty, king of territorial St. Paul's land speculators and neighbor to the Murphys at Sixth and Robert, saw ruin staring him in the face, as did many others. Bankrupt, McKenty was among a number of local speculators who never recovered the fortunes they had amassed during the early 1850s.

The mood was so somber that the arrival of statehood on May 14, 1858, attracted little notice. There were no celebrations. Henry Hastings Sibley was quietly sworn in as Minnesota's first governor. Within the next year, as John and Mary Murphy awaited the birth of their first child, prosperity began a tentative effort to return, but Williams later described a certain sense of forboding: "The disunion cloud was darkening the southern horizon," he wrote, "and the mutterings of war were heard in the distance."

THE SHIELDS GUARDS

Minnesota, as elsewhere in the nation, showed a marked interest in military affairs during the 1850s, perhaps due to the Mexican War of 1846–1847 or the Crimean War of 1853–1856. Communities, especially those near the frontier, formed militia companies, and only partly for protection. Often clad in colorful uniforms— Zouave uniforms patterned after those worn by Algerian troops fighting in the Crimea were popular—the companies marched, paraded, drilled, and organized balls. The Shields Guards was one of them. Organized in St. Paul in 1856 with fifty-two members, it was named for General James Shields, born in County Tyrone, Ireland, and a lawyer, politician, soldier, entrepreneur, who founded Shieldsville, near Faribault in Rice

County. It was Minnesota's first organized Irish community. He was the only senator to be elected to Congress from three separate states: Illinois, Minnesota (elected in 1857), and Missouri. Historian William Watts Folwell describes him as a "soldier of furtune" and "an absurd and irascible Irish politician" but also "a graceful and engaging public speaker possessed of an unusually rich and sonorous voice, which he used with art." Folwell notes that Shields once challenged Abraham Lincoln to "mortal combat in a duel" to protect the honor of a lady thought to be the author of a published bit of doggerel. Lincoln chose cavalry broadswords as weapons and Alton, Illinois, as the site for combat, but cooler heads persuaded Shields to withdraw. Shields died in 1879.

There is no record of what, if any, impact the far-off Civil War or the Dakota Conflict of 1862 on Minnesota's western prairies had on the lives and fortunes of the young Murphy family. In St. Paul the Shields Guards, an all-Irish volunteer company formed in 1856, and the city's Pioneer Guard, another volunteer militia company established a year earlier, were mustered into the First Minnesota Infantry Regiment for service in the Union Army. John Murphy was not among them, nor is he listed on the rosters of any of the other twenty-two military organizations formed in Minnesota during those troubled years of the 1860s. He did not gravitate toward the police force, as did so many of the Irish who were settling in St. Paul (in 1858 six of the eleven officers were Irish); he was not among St. Paul's early firefighters. He appears one final time in recorded history, in the census of 1900, as the father of the little boy baptised in the St. Paul Cathedral in 1864.

John Murphy seems to have remained a laborer, living quietly and probably resourcefully in St. Paul for the rest of his life, which might have been short. There is a family story that the Murphy brothers were "orphaned at an early age." No death certificates, no death notices, no obituaries, no burial records exist for either parent. No handed-down family accounts cast any light on what then happened to the two young boys. Out of St. Paul's 1860 population of 10,279, however almost 3,000 were Irish, either foreign-born or "foreign-mixed." The Murphy brothers' baptismal records list as sponsors Jacobus Murphy, identified as a brother, and Margarita O'Brien, who might have been related to their mother Mary O'Brien. Nothing more is known about them.

Whatever their circumstances, the Murphy sons apparently were not left alone, as Edward himself suggested in later glimpses of his early life. He once said in a newspaper interview that as a boy he attended St. Paul's public schools. Perhaps he was referring to the old Washington School, constructed in 1857 at Ninth and Olive Streets and the first to be built by the city's board of education, or to the Franklin School, which opened in 1865 at Ninth and Broadway. He also said that he dropped out in 1875 when he was twelve years old "to take up market gardening with his parents." At that time, the

---

In 1863, the year the first E. L. Murphy was born . . .

- *The First Minnesota Infantry Regiment, fighting on a hot day in July, lost 215 of its men, dead or wounded during the Battle of Gettysburg. Of the 262 who began the regiment's famous charge on the second day of the battle, July 2, only forty-seven were left to answer the regimental roll call, the greatest loss by a Union regiment during the Civil War. During Pickett's Charge the next day, Marshall Sherman of St. Paul captured the battle flag of the 28th Virginia Regiment. He was awarded the Medal of Honor. The flag remains in the keeping of the Minnesota Historical Society. The following November, in his stirring address dedicating the Gettysburg cemetery, President Abraham Lincoln paid tribute to the men who gave "the last full measure of devotion."*

- *On September 10, 1863, the Third Minnesota Infantry Regiment took part in the capture of Little Rock, Arkansas by Union forces.*

- *Ten days later, on September 20, the 382 men of the Second Minnesota Infantry Regiment suffered forty-five dead, 103 wounded, and fourteen captured while turning back a Confederate attack during the Battle of Chickamauga in Georgia.*

- *Back in St. Paul, in 1863, John Esaias Warren was elected mayor on the Democratic ticket, with 920 votes against J. H. Stewart's 838.*

- *The First National Bank was established on December 8 with J. E. Thompson, president. "This, the pioneer national bank of our State, was one of the earliest established in the country," historian J. Fletcher Williams declared in his 1875 history of Saint Paul.*

- *On December 20 the American House, completed in 1849 at Seven Corners and also known as the Rice House, was destroyed by fire.*

- *The summer season brought a drought that would last into 1864 and produce low water in the Mississippi, seriously affecting trade on the river.*

- *Colonel Henry H. Sibley set out on his expedition to the Missouri River in Dakota Territory, part of a long-running campaign to protect settlements from Indian attacks.*

- *In Minnesota, the Dakota chief Little Crow, and the leader of the Dakota Conflict of 1862, was shot and killed while picking berries with his son in a little glade near Hutchinson. After fleeing into Dakota territory, Little Crow returned to Minnesota, perhaps to find horses.*

equivalent of a sixth grade education was considered entirely adequate and his family evidently needed his help. There is no record of where the Murphy family was living by then, but they might have moved north from Robert "above 6th" after the city's northern limits were extended to Minnehaha in 1872. There also are no records of market garden operations near the city, but the Murphys could have maintained a large home garden and sold their produce at the Market House on Wabasha in downtown St. Paul.

Of Age in a Golden Era

In 1879, when Edward Murphy was sixteen, both he and his brother Jack went to work for (or were apprenticed to) J. F. Eisenmenger, who owned a meat market at 22 East Seventh Street in downtown St. Paul. It must have been a thriving business. By 1886–87, Eisenmenger either had moved to 476 Rice Street or had opened another shop there. It was a time when butcher shops dotted the city, when not everyone had an ice box so housewives shopped several times weekly for food, when meat cut-to-order was the principal item on many menus, and cooks who had never heard of calories, not to mention cholesterol, prepared large meals. After three years with Eisenmenger, Edward Murphy went to work for another butcher, H. J. Meyers, at his shop at 747 Payne Avenue, and two years after that, in 1884 at the age of twenty-one, Murphy bought the shop.

Eisenmenger Meat Market at 455 Wabasha Street in downtown St. Paul. In 1879 when he was sixteen, Edward L. Murphy and his brother Jack, nineteen, went to work, perhaps as apprentices for the Eisenmengers, who, according to the St. Paul City Directory, *operated several meat markets. Minnesota Historical Society photograph.*

He prospered quickly. All his life he would demonstrate the ability to work, to identify opportunity and seize it, but he also had come of age in a golden era, as the 1880s would be known. St. Paul, along with the rest of the country, had emerged from another depression brought on by the Panic of 1873, but that was followed by an economic boom that gilded the 1880s. As the transportation center of a frontier that was being settled rapidly, the growing city was caught up in the beginning of the railroad era in the West.

As times were good, it's scarcely

surprising that Edward Murphy might have felt he was ready to support a wife and establish a family. In January 1883, when he was almost twenty, he married Ellen Brown, five years older than he and also known as Helen and Nellie. Ellen Brown was born in Cincinnati, Ohio, on September 3, 1859, the daughter of Thomas Brown and Bridget Griffith Brown. Like her husband's parents, both of Ellen's parents had been born in Ireland but had paused first in Cincinnati before moving on to Minneapolis.

The following October 1, 1883, the Murphys' first child was born and christened at the Cathedral as Mary Alice Murphy. In 1899 when she was sixteen, Mary Alice joined the Sisters of St. Joseph as Sister Althea Murphy, listing her mother's name as Helen and her godparents as John Murphy and Alice Brown. Eight years later, in 1907, she died of tuberculosis at the age of twenty-four and was buried in the Sisters of St. Joseph plot at Calvary Cemetery in St. Paul.

By 1886 Edward Murphy had settled his family at 608 Farquier (now Bush), not far from his meat market at 747 Payne, but later that year he retired from the meat market business. He opened a saloon at 870 Rice Street and moved his family to 872 Rice, which was either next door or "above the shop." Another daughter, Lillian, was born in 1885; she was followed by a son, Edward Louis Murphy Jr., on August 26, 1888, and by a third daughter, Ella, in 1890. In years to come, Lillian would marry Patrick L. Connolly, who owned a saloon on Jackson Street in downtown St. Paul, and, in 1915, Ella would marry Ibar M. Spellacy. It was a union that would have unforeseen consequences for the Murphy family and firm when, soon after his marriage, Spellacy joined the family firm as vice president.

* * *

In the early 1880s, Edward Murphy's brother Jack was managing a nearby meat market at 899 Rice Street. On November 1, 1888, however, he was appointed a patrolman in the St. Paul Police Department, beginning an on-again-off-again career in what was loosely considered law enforcement. In a system that flourished in many American cities after the Civil War, police work focused on controlling vice, rather than attempting the thankless task of trying to wipe it out.

It's not known why Edward L. Murphy exchanged a meat market for a saloon. In the 1880s, St. Paul had more than 800 saloons; most of them, like Murphy's, were operated by men who ran small businesses that made essential contributions to the economic base of the city. Murphy, the *St. Paul Globe* reported, opened a "buffet," a saloon that served food at its bar. Like many Irish and German entrepreneurs,

Murphy perhaps saw a saloon as a faster route to business success, independence, even political influence, despite the efforts of certain segments of the community to encourage temperance, if not total abstinence.

Whatever lay behind his decision, Murphy must have been a risk-taker. The saloon business was facing determined opposition from a powerful source, Bishop (later archbishop) John Ireland of the Diocese of St. Paul. Taking up the cause of temperance with a vengeance, the bishop launched a campaign in 1886 to dramatically raise the cost of liquor licenses. The move was resisted fiercely by the state's Democratic party, and at some point Murphy came into contact with a man who would be a strong influence on his career. Apparently he had learned early that politics, as well as public employment, were routes to affluence and power and that the Irish in particular were among the power brokers.

Richard T. O'Connor, known as "The Cardinal," was in true turn-of-the-century tradition the Democratic boss of St. Paul and a lieutenant of railroad Empire Builder James J. Hill. According to family lore, the enterprising young Murphy became "one of The Cardinal's buddies." It was a relationship that would have an enormous influence in shaping the young Murphy's career.

It is perhaps unfortunate that Richard O'Connor's reputation has been clouded by his role in the infamous O'Connor System. An arrangement devised to control crime, the system is associated chiefly with the crime-ridden Roaring Twenties, but it actually dated back to the early years of the twentieth century, and it was used in one form or another by other American cities, including Minneapolis. In St. Paul criminals were allowed to remain in town, provided that they registered with the police upon arrival and obeyed the law while there. The short-term goal might have been to make the city safe for its residents, but the long-term results were disastrous—corruption on a scale that finally brought in reformers with the help of the federal government.

Richard O'Connor's brother, John J. O'Connor, who was St. Paul's police chief from 1900 to 1920 and known as "The Big Fellow," is credited with introducing the system into St. Paul. Some historians of the era surmise that the plan actually came from Richard, a rising star in state and national Democratic circles with links to some of the state's most important figures.

The O'Connor brothers were born in Louisville, Kentucky, John in 1855 and Richard in 1857, to Irish immigrant parents who moved their family to St. Paul soon after Richard's birth. Their father, "Honest John"

Richard T. O'Connor, every inch the political boss, also was United States marshal for the District of Minnesota. Sent to Leech Lake in 1898 to serve warrants in connection with the Ojibwe Battle of Sugar Point, O'Connor stopped in at Quam & Drysdale's photo shop in Walker, Minnesota, to have his picture taken. Minnesota Historical Society photograph.

"The Cardinal," Richard T. O'Connor shortly before his death in 1930. Minnesota Historical Society photograph.

O'Connor, was a contractor, hotel proprietor, and Fourth Ward alderman for twenty-five years. Richard was well-educated for that time. He attended Catholic schools in St. Paul until 1870, then St. John's College at Prairie du Chien, Wisconsin, and finally Notre Dame where he graduated from the university's commercial course in 1874.

Back in St. Paul, Richard went to work as an office clerk and collector for James J. Hill's oil, wood and coal business, a valuable connection indeed, since Hill was seen as a behind-the-scenes force for the Democrats. In 1878 O'Connor began to climb the Irish ranks of leadership at city hall. He became deputy city clerk, a position he held for the next nine years even though, in 1883, he was elected Fourth Ward alderman to fill the vacancy created by his father's death. In the fall of 1886 he ran for the position of clerk of district court and was elected to the first of two terms.

It's not surprising that O'Connor rose high and fast in political circles. He had served his apprenticeship under some of Minnesota's most skillful pioneer politicians at a time when the ethnic vote was the key to the control of both the Republican and Democratic parties. As Ann Regan writes in *They Chose Minnesota*, William Pitt Murray, a Scotch-Irish lawyer, was the first to harness the Irish vote. He and Louis Robert, who controlled the French vote, ran the city's Democratic party. Later, as Regan notes, Patrick H. Kelley, a wholesale grocer, and Michael Doran, banker and merchant, took over. Both also were allied with Hill, who seems to have supported, or at least accepted, the O'Connor system, perhaps in the interest of keeping order.

The Battle of Sugar Point

When Grover Cleveland, a Democrat, was elected to his second term as president of the United States in 1892, he appointed Richard O'Connor United States marshal for the District of Minnesota. It was a post that in 1898 led O'Connor into what may have been the last of the long, tragic encounters between United States troops and American Indians, the Battle of Sugar Point at Leech Lake. It was a small battle, hardly dignified by the term—a skirmish, really. It was launched by a handful of Ojibwe who resented indiscriminate arrests of their people by government authorities and felt defrauded of their right to log dead or fallen timber on the Leech Lake reservation. Some shots were fired and the Third Infantry Regiment, stationed at Fort Snelling, marched north. As U. S. marshal, O'Connor accompanied them. When a rifle was fired accidently at Sugar Point, on the northwest side of the lake, more shots rang out and six men were killed. Eventually O'Connor arrested a number of Ojibwe and brought them into Duluth for trial. Leaving his post as marshal in 1899, O'Connor joined several commission and jobber firms in St. Paul's Lowertown, but he remained active in Democratic politics. His friendship with Edward Murphy endured until O'Connor's death on August 11, 1930.

Meanwhile, Murphy was doing well in the saloon business. St. Paul had moved out of its frontier era. Its old frame houses and stubby business blocks were being replaced with often monumental structures typical of that period. A massive combined St. Paul City Hall/ Ramsey County Courthouse was built in 1884 at Fourth and Wabasha Streets, and in 1889 the twelve-story Pioneer Building, the city's first skyscraper, went up at Fourth and Robert. A streetcar line running along Rice Street linked Murphy's North End neighborhood with the city's downtown district.

The 1890 *St. Paul City Directory* continued to list Murphy as a saloonkeeper at 870 Rice but also revealed that he had acquired a second saloon at 20 East Third Street in downtown St. Paul. At about the same time, he moved his family from Rice Street to nearby 77 Front Street (now Front Avenue) and soon opened still another saloon at 524–526 St. Peter Street, advertising it in the 1892 *City Directory* as a "sample room." His

Edward L. Murphy Sr., as a young man, perhaps during the 1890s when he was alderman for St. Paul's Ninth Ward or in the early 1900s when he was a Public Works Commissioner. From Sturdy Sons of St. Paul, *edited by A. R. Fenwich and published in the early 1900s. Minnesota Historical Society photograph from the book.*

brother Jack worked there as a bartender during one of his absences from the police force. In 1896 Edward Murphy made a final move, opening yet another saloon at 345 Wabasha. Located conveniently across the street from the City Hall/County Courthouse, it became a political gathering place.

By this time Murphy had entered politics. Perhaps Richard O'Connor induced him to run for office. As a political boss, O'Connor's interest was in strengthening the Democratic machine by finding capable young candidates to run for public office. Or perhaps Murphy simply followed the Irish bent toward politics. Elected an alderman in 1894, Murphy represented the so-called "bloody Ninth Ward," a North End neighborhood noted for its high-spirited, often contentious residents from various, not always compatible, ethnic backgrounds. Fights were a frequent occurrence.

The neighborhood had been farmland between 1850 and 1857, and its settlement had been slow because of its location two to three miles north of downtown St. Paul. However, by 1872 houses were springing up as the city annexed the area. St. Patrick's Church was founded in 1884 and it became the Murphy family's church. The North End was a working class neighborhood settled by German, Irish, and Swedish immigrants who found jobs in the Jackson Street railroad yards and other area industries. Eastern European immigrants, particularly Romanians, joined them and a Jewish community established itself beyond the ridge where a new state Capitol would be built.

Ninth Ward voters must have seen Murphy as a forceful representative on the Common Council, as it was known then. A physically imposing man, as was his brother, he was over six feet tall and weighed more than 200 pounds. There are family stories of how he fought off attempts by the city to raise the license fees of the Ninth Ward's Jewish peddlers. An undated biographical sketch of Murphy, published around 1900 in a small book titled *Sturdy Sons of Saint Paul*, summed up his career as an alderman and his subsequent defeat in admiring terms:

> He has three times been a candidate for alderman from the
> Ninth Ward and has been twice elected, his defeat coming at
> his second running, though he only lost by thirty votes when
> the general Democratic ticket was turned down with 3,800
> against it.

Describing him as "naturally a leader, owing to his sagacity and self poise, as well as his fairness in the treatment of men and policies," the book also noted that "his service as alderman has marked him as a forceful man and he has made the record of being the champion of measures tending to promote the general public welfare."

A glimpse of Murphy's political manuevering can be seen in a brief item in the *St. Paul Dispatch* in 1893:

> The Board of Aldermen was to have met yesterday afternoon but Alderman Murphy, for some mysterious reason, secured an adjournment until this evening. It has been learned that his reason for doing so was that the Democrats might have time in which to inquire into the law as to the appointment of ballot judges. Murphy wanted to see if the appointment had to be a joint action or whether the board could make the appointments irrespective of the assembly, and a commission is now looking up the law. If it has to be a joint action, the scheme will fall through, as the assembly on Monday night will sit down hard upon the proposition. If the board of aldermen can act independently, then it will be snap judgment upon the Republicans, who sent in no list of ballot judges.

An 1896 view north from Wabasha Street before construction of the new Capitol began. The magnificent Merriam House, built in 1882 by Governor William Merriam (1889–1893), looms above the store sign on the right. Beyond the distant ridge lay the Ninth Ward with its Jewish constituency that E. L. Murphy Sr., served as city alderman. St. Paul Dispatch-Pioneer Press photograph, Minnesota Historical Society collections.

(In the rough and tumble politics of those years, with ballots marked by hand, ballot judges could be the key to a successful election on the part of one or another party's candidate.)

When Murphy left office as an alderman, his Jewish constituents gave him a massive handcarved oak liquor cabinet that remains in the family. Another family memento from those years is a gold-headed cane dated 1898 and inscribed "To E. L. Murphy from his Ninth Ward Friends." Despite his loss at the polls, he remained in politics. In 1901 he was appointed to the Board of Public Works Commissioners, where he served until 1910.

Among Murphy's strengths, during his sixteen years as alderman and Public Works commissioner, was his ability to provide jobs for the many working men who were pouring into the neighborhood on the crest of one of the last great immigration booms of the turn-of-the-century. They were jobs that were sorely needed after another disastrous depression settled in following the Panic of 1893. It is not difficult to imagine the power wielded by such men as Murphy and his fellow aldermen and Public Works commissioners. They were part of a system that ran many American cities at that time. As aldermen they would review requests for public works projects, approve the requests, and send them on to the Public Works board. As Public Works commissioners, Murphy and his colleagues would investigate the approved projects, decide whether or not the "improvements" were "proper and necessary" and, if so, send the Common Council "a proper order directing that the work be done."

The North End

In 1886 when Edward L. Murphy opened his saloon at 870 Rice Street, nearly all of the North End south of Maryland Avenue had been settled, developed by owners of small businesses who purchased sections of land on speculation and subdivided them into lots. Three large cemeteries also were established there: Oakland, founded in 1853 as a city cemetery and planned by the famous architect, Horace W. S. Cleveland; Elmhurst, established in 1865 as a German Lutheran cemetery; and Calvary, a Catholic cemetery founded in 1866. In years to come Murphy would purchase a plot there for his family.

Along the southern fringe of the North End, at Dale and Rice streets and not far from Murphy's home on Front Street, were the tracks, shops, and lumber yards of the St. Paul, Minneapolis and Manitoba railroad, soon to be James J. Hill's Great Northern. Nearby, Austrian and German immigrants, responding to the railroad's need for workers, built small homes and kept much of their language and customs intact. In the 1890s, Murphy would represent them, as well as others in his working class contituency as a St. Paul alderman.

Murphy and other public officials were presiding over a city that was in the grip of massive change as the infrastructure of a modern metropolis gradually emerged. It is clear from the old records in the St. Paul Public Works Department that as an alderman Murphy took care of his own. It was resolved by the Council, for example, that the Department of Public Works sprinkle the streets from Front Street to Maryland during the summer season and that a wooden sidewalk be constructed on the west side of Mississippi Street from Granite. He offered a resolution asking that a drinking fountain be placed on the east side of Rice Street at the intersection of University Avenue and another on the east side of Rice Street thirty feet south of Wayzata. All these projects were in the Ninth Ward.

Throughout the city, sewers were being installed, streets were being laid out or paved, wooden sidewalks were being repaired and relaid, and gas lamps were being moved from one corner to another to accomodate changes in neighborhoods. According to Public Works records, Murphy voted on June 17, 1898, to approve "rebuilding the present sidewalks on both sides of Cook Street, between Payne and Greenbrier" in the Ninth Ward. In 1894, 223 payments were issued "for laying cement walks" and $355,698 was spent for sewers and paving bridges.

Other matters caught the aldermen's eyes. The Spanish-American War had broken out in April 1898. The following October 6 the council voted to pay $500 out of its Emergency Fund for supplies fur-

Minnesota state Capitol construction scene around 1898. Jack Murphy hauled stone to the Capitol site before selling two of his horses and a wagon to his brother. Minnesota Historical Society photograph.

nished to volunteers in the United States army and navy who were "going to their destinations from St. Paul."

Murphy, Shiely, and the New Capitol

It was the major construction project of the 1890s and early 1900s in St. Paul, the building of the new state Capitol, that was the impetus that almost accidentally led Murphy into an entirely new endeavor. Even though he would remain a saloonkeeper and a politician for a few more years, the trucking business would occupy him for the rest of his life. Construction of the Capitol, designed by St. Paul architect Cass Gilbert, began in 1896 and was spread over the next ten years. As a saloonkeeper and a successful businessman, a North End alderman, and trusted associate of Richard T. O'Connor, Edward Murphy could well have been a player in that important project. A family story maintains that Murphy snared a contract to haul building materials to the site, although his name does not appear in the Capitol construction records. Joseph L. Shiely, son of a teamster and founder in 1914 of today's J. L. Shiely Construction Company, is listed as the general hauling contractor, but Murphy, according to the story, had a hand in that through his association with O'Connor. Irishmen both, Shiely and Murphy must have known each other. (Down the years, a Murphy grandson would marry a Shiely granddaughter.) As one family member observed, "It was common knowledge that if you wanted some of the work that was out there, the O'Connors would have something to say about who was going to do it."

THE FATE OF THREE CAPITOLS

St. Paul's first Capitol dated back to the creation of Minnesota Territory in 1849. At the time, the newly appointed government met at the Central House, a hotel on the corner of Minnesota and Second Street, a site just above the steamboat landing at the foot of Jackson Street. Legislative sessions were held wherever space could be found in the small community.

The government, however, found a permanent home when the territorial Capitol was built in 1853 at Tenth and Wabasha for $31,223. In 1881 the building burned to the ground in a fire of unknown origin. The government moved to the Market House at Sixth and Wabasha while a new Capitol was built, at a cost of $275,000, on the site of the earlier Capitol. Finally, work began in 1898 on the $2 million present state Capitol for which Jack Murphy hauled stone. The teams and wagons he used he would sell to his brother as the first assets of what became the Murphy Transfer Company.

About the time work on the Capitol began, Murphy's brother Jack, who was not on the police force between 1896 and 1901, invested in the first of several wagons and teams of horses, and possibly it was Jack, not his brother, who was among some independent teamsters hauling stone to the Capitol site. His name does not appear in the records, either, but he might have been hired on an informal, handshake basis.

For the next decade, Jack Murphy moved in and out of the St. Paul Police Department, a comfortable relationship that again, family stories maintain, was due to E. L. Murphy's connection with the O'Connor brothers. While the records are sketchy, they do indicate that Jack Murphy was first appointed to the police force in 1888 and resigned in 1891; he was reappointed in 1895, but resigned again a year later; he was reappointed in 1901 and resigned in 1902. He is listed for the next several years as an inspector for the Public Works department, perhaps due to his brother, who by this time was a Public Works commissioner. He was reappointed to the police force in 1908 and assigned to mounted duty, but resigned again eight months later.

Finally, in 1910 he was reappointed for the last time. In 1913 he was assigned to motorcycle duty and promoted to sergeant the following year. After that he remained with the police force until he retired and was placed on pension, although department records list both 1930 and 1934 as his retirement date. For some of those years he worked out of the Prior Avenue station. He lived for many years with the rest of the Murphys on Front Street, across from or next to his younger brother, and in 1934, when he was seventy-four years old, he died at the home of his daughter in Duluth.

With his death, Jack Murphy disappears from this story, but his importance to it lies with his ownership of the teams and wagons that his brother bought. In 1953 Edward L. Murphy Jr., wrote out his own brief account of the founding in 1904 of what became the Murphy Transfer Company. He noted that his father "bought 2 horses and a wagon from Jack Murphy," and that was the move that marked the senior Murphy's entry into the drayage or teaming business, as it was known then.

Just why Murphy decided to go into the drayage business is just as unknown as why he moved from a meat market to a saloon. Basically, he was a politician, but he also was an entrepreneur. He was well-connected in the liquor industry, he was closely associated with Richard T. O'Connor and the other leaders of the Democratic party, and he had formed friend-

ONLY TWO CARS

In 1900, according to the St. Paul Dispatch, *only two cars and two trucks were owned by city residents. From* The Minnesota Book of Days: An Almanac of State History *(Minnesota Historical Society Press, 2001).*

The Murphy Transfer Company hauling heavy machinery around 1919 when the company's name was changed to Murphy Transfer & Storage Company.

ships with St. Paul community and business leaders that would prove invaluable in years to come. As a transportation and distribution center for the Northwest, St. Paul beckoned with opportunity. In 1904 there were only 700 trucks in all of the United States. An enterprising businessman might have noted that, as a few automobiles began to appear on the streets of St. Paul, somewhere in the future lay the end of horse-drawn transport, overtaken by the arrival of the internal combustion engine on which the senior Murphy would base the rest of his career.

In any event, in 1904 his son, Edward L. Murphy Jr. was sixteen years old and it was time to consider his future. The younger Murphy had attended Mechanic Arts High School before being sent off to Notre Dame University, which has recorded his presence but not his course or any years of study there.

Later he would tell with some relish the story of his brief and checkered career at Notre Dame. He seems to have fought his way through higher education. He once described an argument he had with a Notre Dame priest that ended with both priest and student repairing to the gymnasium to settle the dispute with boxing gloves. After the young Murphy had been royally trounced, he was expelled and sent back to St. Paul. According to one of his daughters, he then apparently attended either Cretin High School or St. Thomas Academy, with the same result: expelled after a fight with a priest. In any event, his first job, he once said, was running a freight elevator. Many years later he told the *St. Paul News* that he had dreamed of becoming a lawyer but he went to work instead for his father. In his words, he "accepted the gift" of those two horses and the wagon from his father and was assigned to drive the wagon. The company's office was in the Murphy home on Front Street and its first account was Works Biscuit, later absorbed by the Loose-Wiles Company. Some twenty years later, E. L. Murphy Jr., remembered how he drove the wagon for Works Biscuit:

> I got $125 a month for myself, the horses and the wagon and they had their company's name on the wagon, too. I fed the horses. And they never closed the freight houses on me evenings. In those days you worked until you were done, which was often 9 or 9:30 at night.

Horses and wagons lined up outside the Murphys' Minneapolis warehouse. The sign indicates the points served by the trucking company around the time of World War I.

Leaving the Works Biscuit Company, he hauled "where it pleased him and where the pay was best." This led him into a confrontation with friends from Mechanic Arts. As he recalled it, he was shoveling sand to haul from an excavation for the old Northern Heating Company at Fifth and Robert Streets when he encountered a crowd of former schoolmates who had found jobs in the general offices of the Great Northern Railroad (later the Burlington Northern building) at the corner of Fifth and Robert.

"Did you have to go to Notre Dame to learn how to shovel?" they taunted him. Murphy kept on shoveling. "I knew that gang," he said.

"If I had started an argument they'd have collected a crowd and begun razzing me in earnest."

Four More Teams

In 1905, as business began to look promising, E. L. Murphy Sr., bought four more teams from his brother Jack. After paying expenses, all else that was earned went back into the business. In 1907 the company opened its first real office—desk space in the N. W. Employment Agency office at 188 East Third Street, across from the venerable Merchants Hotel. Harry Herman at the agency answered their phone. Other early accounts were T. L. Blood, who sold paints and varnishes, on the southwest corner of Fourth and Wabasha; Foley Brothers, wholesale grocers, at 312–322 Broadway; Noyes Bros. & Cutler, wholesale druggists, at Sixth and Sibley; Carnation Milk; and Griggs-Cooper at 133 East Third Street.

In 1908 the *St. Paul City Directory* published the first listing of the company as the E. L. Murphy Company, with E. L. Murphy Jr. as foreman and boarding at the family home on Front Street. Edward Jr., however, seems to have taken over the fledgling family transport business. His 1953 handwritten notes describing the company's earliest years are unclear as to the roles of father and son. However, since Edward Sr., remained a Public Works commissioner until 1910, it is highly probable that, as the family story goes, he provided the money and the contacts and Edward Jr., did the work. In 1909 the company moved into offices of its own in an old house at Ninth and Temperance streets on property owned by the H. M. Smyth Company, an early St. Paul printing firm. Edward Jr., remembered that there were furniture pads on the floor, that he often slept there, and that he could call the "telephone company and ask them to call [me] at 6 a.m."

The young firm focused on city deliveries, which meant many trips to and from the railroad freight yards and the wholesale companies crowding the Lowertown business district. Heavy hauling started about this time, too, with the Diebold Safe and Lock Company at 350–352 Jackson Street, as its first such account. The Murphys built a machinery wagon. The trucking industry had greeted the dawn of the automobile age with small, local delivery vans powered by steam, electricity, gas, even compressed air, but in 1910 the Murphys introduced what might have been the first motorized trucks into St. Paul. By 1912 the company had moved to Third and Sibley, across the street from the old St. Paul Union Depot, and as it continued to grow (five teams and ten employees that year), it moved again to 175 East Eighth Street in 1915.

Like many businessmen in an era when workers faced long hours, low wages and little job security, the Murphys laid down strict rules. The following "Notice to All Teamsters" was posted on May 5, 1911:

> Hereafter, all teamsters must report at the barn on Sundays to take care of their teams and have all work done by nine-thirty a.m. If driver is not at the barn by eight-thirty, he can stay away. We will have work done and he will be fined fifty cents which will be collected or taken out of his wages. Further, if any driver in our employment is not satisfied with this rule, he can quit. We have been abused enough in this manner and it is an injustice to those who carry out these rules. To break rules is a thing that must not be allowed in the future.

A lineup of thirteen A. C. Mack trucks outside the Murphy Transfer office in 1916.

Although the Murphys obviously ran a tight ship, their relationship with their workers during these early years remains unknown. Unions had reached out to Minnesota's workers as early as the 1850s, but the International Brotherhood of Teamsters wasn't formed until 1899. No family stories have surfaced to indicate that the relationship was particularly adversarial, suggesting that the company, although a union shop, was spared some of the bitterness that marred management and labor affairs in a rapidly industrializing America.

St. Paul was a closed-shop city and labor relations were less contentious than in many other American cities, as Mary Lethert Wingerd has pointed out in *Claiming the City,* her fine study of "Politics, Faith, and the Power of Place in St. Paul," published by Cornell University Press (2001). She writes that St. Paul valued civic solidarity, that there was a sense of loyalty to the community, a history of negotiating labor problems, rather than taking them to the streets.

At right: Edward L. Murphy Sr.'s home at 77 Front Street (now Front Avenue). He moved his family here in the 1890s and, with his son, opened the company's first office here. After their marriage in 1912, Edward Jr., and Frances Tenner Murphy lived first with the senior Murphys, then moved next door (left) to 73 Front Street. Their children remember playing in the spacious side yard between the two houses. Photos by Susan Lightfoot for the Murphy Warehouse Company.

While labor strife was not unknown in St. Paul, it remained muted until workers did take to the streets in the bitter streetcar strike of 1917. Streetcar motormen, defying the Twin City Rapid Transit Company's ban on union employees, struck in October, only six months after America's entrance into World War I. The Minnesota Home Guard, deputized by Governor J. A. A. Burnquist to keep order after the state's National Guard troops were sworn into federal service, appeared on the downtown streets of St. Paul. Rioting by "uncontrolled wild mobs," numbering in the thousands, according to excited news reports, had stopped trolley service. "A score of persons were arrested." Streetcar windows were smashed and conductors and motormen were stoned. Stranded cars, their windows smashed, were abandoned on downtown streets. During the four-hour fray, the press reported, the downtown streets rang with shouts of the mob, and rioters captured a number of car crews at Robert and Wabasha. Finally the Home Guard established order.

* * *

Edward L. Murphy Jr. and Frances Tenner on their wedding day in 1912.

In 1912 Edward Jr., then twenty-four, married Frances Tenner, whose parents had emigrated from Switzerland and whose father had a barber shop on East Seventh Street. They would have five children: Genevieve, born in 1913; a third Edward L. Murphy, born in 1915 who in turn would become E. L. Murphy Jr. and be known as Ed (or "Bud" in the family); Dorothie, born in 1918; Althea in 1920, and Richard Tenner Murphy, born in 1924. Known as Dick, he was named for the senior Murphy's great friend, Richard T. O'Connor. Both sons would join the family firm. For a short time the new Murphy family lived with the groom's parents at 77 Front Street, then next door at 73 Front. (They moved again in 1915 to a duplex at 1032 Dayton Avenue, and yet again two years later to 694 Grand Avenue).

On October 8, 1913, the Murphy Transfer Company was, according to its legal documents, "duly organized under the laws of the State of Minnesota for a period of thirty years to do a general transfer and storage business." Edward Murphy Sr., was president and treasurer and Edward Jr., secretary. The company's authorized, outstanding capital was $30,000, consisting of 300 shares of common stock having a value of $100 per share. Its assets were the wagons, teams, and trucks of its drayage business. Now listed at 475 Temperance in Lowertown, with E. L. Murphy Jr., as manager, the company's ad in the *St. Paul City Directory* carried the helpful notice: "Transfer and General Machinery Moving a Specialty." Stock was issued: 164 shares to Edward Sr.; 125 to Edward Jr.; 10 shares to I. M Spellacy; and 1 share to Ellen Murphy, E. L. Sr.'s wife. Annual meetings were set for the second Monday in October of each year.

A year later the company launched into the business of "overland hauling" to Minneapolis, then considered an "overland" trip. As a newspaper account described it, "the condition of University Avenue in those days made the trip something of an adventure."

In the next few years, the Murphys assembled their trucking fleet.

Ellen Murphy's certificate for her one share of stock issued by the Murphy Transfer Company upon its incorporation in 1913.

By 1916 they owned twenty-six red and yellow rigs known famously as "Murphy's circus wagons." Their wheels and frame were painted yellow and the super structure red with the Murphy name in gold leaf on the sides.

As the company continued to grow, E. L. Murphy Sr., retired from politics, stepping down as a Public Works commissioner to devote all his time to the trucking business and his widespread community contacts that helped nurture it. His friends and business associates included Otto and Adolf Bremer, brewers, bankers, and major shareholders in the American National Bank, organized in 1903 by a group of bankers and businessmen that included Otto Bremer. It became known as "the Bremer bank," and the Murphys would bank there until 1935. The next step

The company's ad in the 1919 St. Paul City Directory featuring the famed Murphy "circus wagon." Lettering on top was gold leaf against red; the wheels and frame were yellow. It's appropriate that the ad shared space with the majestic Ryan Hotel where the Murphys and their cronies often gathered.

forward came in 1919 when at its annual meeting in October the company legally changed its name. All assets of the Murphy Transfer Company were "sold" for $30,000 to the company that henceforth would be known as Murphy Transfer & Storage Company. At that time the firm was still operating locally, transfering goods from railroad to warehouse, but as its new name suggests, the "transfer" side of the business was continuing to drive the "storage" side.

2

Surviving Hard Times

A S THE 1920S ARRIVED, the *Minneapolis Journal* declared that the nation had "earned a rest." It was the Roaring Twenties, the Jazz Age, the "flapper era," a period known for its extravagance and its economic boom and bust. High production, high employment, and stable prices nurtured a state of euphoria as many of St. Paul's people found themselves comfortably prosperous, well-to-do, even rich. It was not entirely a restful period, however, as Americans feverishly pursued some of the pleasures that had been denied them during the grim years of World War I, and for some it was a frightening decade.

St. Paul, whose population had grown to 234,698, was entering a period of turmoil. The great figures who had dominated the city's history for almost sixty years were dead, James J. Hill in 1916 and Archbishop John Ireland in 1918. Michael Gebhart succeeded John J. O'Connor as police chief at O'Connor's death in 1920. For Richard T. O'Connor, now immersed in national Democratic politics, death would follow in 1930. According to historian Mary Lethert Wingerd, labor, bruised by the streetcar strike, was moving from a conservative to activist stance.

An agricultural depression had settled in and St. Paul's banking community was washed by the ripples of failures by country banks with their frozen paper and their close ties to large city banks. As James B. Bell writes in his history of Norwest Bank St. Paul, published in *Ramsey County History* (Fall 1995), "farmers had over-extended and over-produced, lured into believing that the World War I-induced demand for grain and livestock would continue indefinitely. In the land boom, financed largely by the region's small, rural banks, the agricultural bust was dramatic."

During the 1920s, 2,333 banks in the Upper Midwest failed. Bank examiners swooped down on a number of troubled St. Paul banks with the result that they were shored up only by mergers with, or emergency financial transfusions from, larger and stronger banks. In St. Paul, in 1924, the Capital Trust & Savings Bank, an affiliate of Capital National Bank, failed. It was the worst bank failure in the city's history, Bell writes—so serious that a group of worried St. Paul bankers rushed in with a dead-of-night rescue. On the night of May 4, a truck under heavy guard moved Capital's books and assets from its vault to that of Merchants National Bank. Two years later when St. Paul's National Exchange Bank was teetering on the brink of closing, local bankers raised $350,000 to keep it afloat. In 1929 it would change its name to the Exchange Bank.

No family stories, no company records suggest that any of this economic turmoil touched Murphy Transfer & Storage. Goods still had to be hauled by truck from railroad to warehouse. Not for long did Edward Murphy Sr., continue to live on Front Street in St. Paul's aging North End. In 1923, his children married, he bought a house at 1774 Stanford, the first "all electric" house in St. Paul. All the appliances

Edward L. Murphy Sr.'s, "all electric" house at 1774 Stanford Avenue, St. Paul where he moved in 1923. Photographed in 2002 by Susan Lightfoot for the Murphy Warehouse Company.

were electric. It was, as granddaughter Carole Murphy Faricy described it, "The first house I'd ever been in where you entered in the middle and the stairs went all the way up to the roof. And there was another stairway that went up from the kitchen to the bedrooms above. I thought that was the biggest deal I'd ever seen." It is interesting to note that this son of an Irish immigrant chose for his new home a Spanish-inspired design by architect Percy Dwight Bentley.

In 1925, E. L. Murphy Jr., moved his family to a house at 118 Exeter Place, close to the St. Thomas University campus. This far western section of the affluent Merriam Park neighborhood, the last of that area of St. Paul to be developed, is still studded with fine examples of Period Revival architectural styles popular in the 1920s. Murphy's elegant two-story home, with its red-tiled roof, arched windows, and iron grillwork over the front door, reflected the same popular Spanish influence that had appealed to his father.

The senior Murphy seems to have caught the spirit of the times, after years of building the trucking business and wheeling and dealing in Richard T. O'Connor's political arena. (Carole Faricy remembered that her grandfather and his colleagues were known around City Hall as "the big deals.") Murphy bought a yellow convertible with red wire wheels and he would take his grandchildren for spins. "In those days a convertible was really unique," grandson Richard T. Murphy remembered.

He fell in love with the movies. He would go the movies "three or four times a week," grandson Edward L. "Ed" Murphy recalled. "On Friday nights he would always take us to a movie someplace. He took in the stage shows at the old Metropolitan and the Orpheum, the most opulent of the downtown theaters, but he never played cards." It was the era of the silent film: Pola Negri in *Passion;* Charlie Chaplin; the years when Mary Pickford was "America's Sweetheart" and movie theater tickets were 10 cents.

E. L. Murphy Sr., and his wife Ellen began spending winters in southern California, in Hollywood or Los Angeles. For a time they drove the long distance. Ellen Murphy once described the trips—how he would tire, drive off the road into a field and nap for a time while she sat patiently waiting for him to wake up and resume their journey. Later, grandchildren took over the driving.

He bought a summer cabin at Lake Minnewawa, near McGregor, Minnesota. "We never realized how much our grandfather did for us," Ed Murphy said. "He did it so quietly." Those years at Lake Minnewawa, however, have produced conflicting memories among his grandchildren. The cabin was typical of the years of "roughing it" at

Ellen Murphy, (top left) with five of her grandchildren at Lake Minnewawa, near McGregor, Minnesota, in the mid-1920s. The baby is Richard Murphy; Ed Murphy stands behind him. In front are Dorothie (left), Althea, and Genevieve.

lake homes with neither electricity nor indoor plumbing. There was one bedroom, a big porch that surrounded the house, and an outhouse in back. The Murphy grandchildren, overseen by their grandmother Ellen Murphy, spent much of the summer there. "Grandmother was a terrible cook," Carole Faricy remembered. "She made terrible pancakes, but she was a sweetheart. She was good to us. She never disciplined us. She loved being a mom again."

"I'd get out of St. Mark's school in June and within days I'd be on my way up to the lake with my siblings," Dick Murphy recalled. "We'd stay until school started in the fall. All of the grandchildren spent the entire summer there when we were young. My older sister Dorothie and I just loved the place, even though I never learned to fish."

His brother remembered that those trips introduced them to their grandfather's long-ago skill as a butcher. "When we'd ride up to McGregor with him in the spring, he'd go into Batchelor's store, march back to the cooler, and pick out the meat he wanted. He knew his meat." Ed Murphy also recalled that,

I never saw grandmother go near the water. I don't remember ever seeing her in a boat. I don't think she knew one end of a fishing pole from the other. Grandpa spent a limited amount of time there. I never saw him in the water or in a boat, either, and he was no fisherman. My father liked that lake place even less. Whenever he went up there, he got out as fast as he could. Grandma Murphy loved it and Grandpa Murphy hated it.

Still, the family tradition of summer at Lake Minnewawa endured until the outbreak of World War War II. Meanwhile, the 1920s marked the development of the Murphys' storage business, a natural outgrowth of trucking. Murphy Transfer & Storage Company's major business, however, remained local cartage and the hauling of heavy machinery.

Warehouses in Both Cities

In 1923 the company borrowed $125,000 from Northwestern National Bank in Minneapolis and the following year built a warehouse at 400 North Fourth Street in the Minneapolis warehouse district.

Murphy's employees lined up in front of the St. Paul warehouse built in 1927. Of the four men standing in back on the right, Ibar Spellacy is the man in the light hat and dark glasses; Edward L. Murphy Sr., is wearing a dark coat and E. L. Murphy Jr., a light coat. The dispatcher known fondly as "Around the Corner" Folska is the tall man on the far right. The young girl (front row) in the light coat is Genevieve Murphy.

Both Murphys, senior and junior, had connections in Minneapolis. Their cartage business required the moving of freight from depots in Minneapolis to wholesale houses between the two cities and in the Lowertown district of St. Paul. Another factor was the presence as a company officer of Ibar Spellacy, E. L. Murphy Sr.'s, son-in-law. After his marriage to Ella Murphy, Spellacy worked for the company as manager of "a little hole-in-the wall" office in Minneapolis while the Murphys based the company's operations in St. Paul.

In 1927 they built a second warehouse, this time in St. Paul. It was a carbon copy of the Minneapolis building. As the company's first Minute Book reported: "Built warehouse on lots 3, 4, 5, 13, Kittson's addition." The address was Ninth and Broadway. On May 27 of that year, the minutes noted another loan: $220,000 from American National Bank, to pay off the company's 1923 indebtedness incurred in building the Minneapolis warehouse and to finance the new warehouse in St. Paul. The loan was secured by a mortgage on the two properties. A news story in the February 24, 1927, issue of the *St. Paul Daily News* described the plans for the St. Paul warehouse:

> A $200,000 five-story motor truck terminal building is to be erected in St. Paul by the Murphy Transfer & Storage Co. It will be the most modern truck terminal in the west, making St. Paul the center of motor truck business in this region, according to Col. Lewis H. Brittin, industrial director of the St. Paul Association. The building will be located between 9th and 10th sts., facing Broadway and will be served by Great Northern trackage. Contracts for its construction will be let immediately.
>
> This will be the headquarters for the Murphy Transfer & Storage Co. and the Judson Freight Forwarding Co., which this week initiated its free store delivery service of consolidated car shipments.
>
> The building will contain about 70,000 square feet of floor space. It is 220 feet long by 190 feet wide, the main part of it, not counting the wings, containing about 100 [*sic*] square feet. It is to be built of reinforced concrete and will be fireproof.

Three generations: Ed Murphy (Edward L. Murphy III) left; his father and grandfather.

The trucks will be loaded and unloaded in an immense basement which will serve as a garage for the fleet of trucks belonging to the transfer company. They will be lowered into the basement by a powerful ramp.

The Murphy Transfer & Storage Co. already has started interstate truck service, running a line from St. Paul to Eau Claire, Wis. The consolidated car shipments now are being handled by the Judson Freight Forwarding Co. through three sections of the Great Northern terminal leased for that purpose until the terminal is completed. Negotiations for the site were handled through Col. Brittin, who proposed a truck terminal last summer in connection with the University ave. expansion program. The trackage facilities at the building will have a capacity of 10 freight cars.

Ed Murphy was twelve years old in 1927 and remembered the St. Paul warehouse. One account "was Studebaker cars shipped to St. Paul from South Bend, Indiana, unloaded, stored in the warehouse, then sold and moved out again. Another was sugar. Prohibition was in force and there always was some suspicion that the sugar stored in the warehouse was used to make rum and other bootleg liquor, but it was there and it went to anyone who needed it, including those in the bootlegging business, I suppose." General merchandise also flowed

Four of the Murphy men: Ed Murphy, second from left, with his father, left, his grandfather, and his uncle, Jack Murphy, on the right, in the early 1920s. This seems to be the only surviving picture of Jack Murphy whose "2 horses and a wagon" launched the Murphy Transfer Company.

into the warehouses. The A&P Tea company shipped in boxcars of groceries from Milwaukee; the cars would be unloaded at the warehouses and the groceries distributed to A&P stores throughout Minnesota and Wisconsin.

Dick Murphy remembered the company barn on L'Orient Street, up the road from the warehouse on Broadway. Although Murphy Transfer had introduced motorized trucks into St. Paul before World War I, the company continued to use some horse-drawn wagons until the 1930s.

> I remember going as a youngster with my father to the barn after mass on Sunday and there the teamsters would be caring for the horses. When I was older, I'd sometimes ride on the wagon with some of the teamsters as they went between the freight houses in downtown St. Paul and along University Avenue to Minneapolis and the freight houses there. It was a thrill to spend a day sitting in the wagon.

Hard rubber tires on metal wheels—heavy hauling in the 1920s.

In an era that was rich with promise, the Murphys had positioned their company in the center of an expanding transportation network. Despite the agricultural depression, out in Minnesota's countryside farm products still had to be sold and supplies bought. Murphy trucks hauled milk, eggs, butter, cheese, meat, and poultry from farm to market and brought hardware, produce, and groceries back to country storekeepers. The trips often were hazardous. In spite of the advent of the Federal Road Act of 1916 and the Good Roads movement, highways were not just poor, they also were poorly maintained, and the country roads frequently were little more than two-lane gravel

One of the Murphy trucks around 1927.

tracks pockmarked with holes. There were few signs, guide posts, or traffic lights. Road maps were creative, often directing a driver to "turn left" at a red barn that long since had burned down. Since many roads were snow-clogged during the winter, the Murphys equipped their trucks with plows to clear the routes. According to company stories, when word got around a community that a plow-equipped Murphy truck was on its way, people would gather to follow it in and out of town. Breakdowns were common, truck cabs were unheated, and shock absorbers had not yet been invented. Tires often were hard rubber, even though balloon tires had been introduced around 1923.

In 1925 the Murphys took steps to insure the company's future. A life insurance policy in the amount of $20,000 was issued on the life of Edward L. Murphy Sr. Again peering into the future, the Murphys began to purchase more property for expansion purposes. In Minneapolis they owned several lots in addition to their warehouse, as well as other property nearby.

Trucking was becoming big business, but it could be dangerous and fraught with accident, at least once tragically for the Murphy company. A 1920s newspaper article described how a seven-year-old school boy was hit by a Murphy Transfer Company truck. The boy was crossing University Avenue at Virginia on his way home from St. Vincent's school. Seeing a line of school children crossing University under the protection of the St. Paul school police, the truck's driver, only nineteen years old himself, tried frantically to stop. His brakes apparently failed; the truck ran through the school police stop signal.

The boy, who evidently tried to save himself by hanging onto the front of the truck, lost his grip, fell under the wheels, and was killed. A subsequent investigation determined that the truck might have been overloaded.

The Dawning of Regulation

By the mid-1920s, some form of regulation already was being considered for an industry that in its freewheeling state could be chaotic and sometimes unstable. The end of World War I had unleashed thousands of war-surplus vehicles, accelerating the end of horse-drawn wagons as horses became too expensive to house and feed. More than three million trucks were on the nation's roadways. Anyone with enough money to buy a truck could enter the hauling business, set his own rates, compete for the best routes, and ignore those less profitable. Cut-throat competition ruled to the extent that established companies could be undercut and the industry's economics upset.

A Murphy Motor Freight Lines truck-trailer at American Hoist & Derrick on St. Paul's West Side. The trailer's tires are hard rubber but the truck is fitted with pneumatic tires.

The Minnesota Legislature introduced an early form of regulation of the state's trucking industry in 1925. The new law required truckers to have certificates issued by the Minnesota Railroad and Warehouse Commission in order to carry freight from one point to another. Trucking companies not only had to apply for authority to haul the freight, but also prove a need to do so and wait for the Commission to approve or not. The political skills Edward L. Murphy Sr., had honed during his long years in politics "were very helpful," Ed Murphy observed. Murphy Transfer & Storage was certified for hauling to Winona, Willmar, Mankato, and Faribault.

Trucking industry leaders thought they saw the competitive muscle of the railroads behind this and later attempts at regulation. The railroads, they felt, supported regulation as a means of subduing, if not killing, the trucking companies that were challenging them and turning the Twin Cities' Midway district into the fourth largest trucking center in the country. "The railroads' method," said one industry

Heavy hoisting in 1935.

leader, "was to promote truck regulation in Minnesota. Their theory was that 'we will control it by having nobody in business without a certificate and we will control who gets the certificates.'" The struggle could be vicious at times. Keys were pulled out of parked trucks and thrown away. Drivers were harassed by the police. It would be many years before the trucking companies and the railroads joined forces in "piggybacking" their cargoes.

Another competitor also arrived. In 1926 Northwest Airlines was organized and awarded an air mail contract; passenger and freight express soon were added. Holman field opened across the Mississippi from downtown St. Paul; Wold-Chamberlain field was operating

A White truck, part of the Murphy Transfer & Storage fleet in the 1920s—red on top with gold lettering, yellow on the bottom. The truck burned up in 1928.

THE FIRST THREE GENERATIONS

Generation 1

John Murphy, born in Ireland, date unknown; married Mary O'Brien, also born in Ireland, date unknown; emigrated to America, date unknown. Settled in St. Paul before 1856-1857, as listed in a city directory.

Their children were: John Murphy, born in St. Paul, September 19, 1860

Edward Louis Murphy, born in St. Paul, April 15, 1863

Generation 2

Edward Louis Murphy married Ellen M. Brown, born in Cincinnati, Ohio, September 3, 1859; daughter of Thomas Brown and Bridget Brown, both born in Ireland, dates unknown.

Their children were: Mary Alice Murphy, born October 1, 1883 (joined Sisters of St. Joseph in 1899 at age 16; died 1907 of tuberculosis)

Lillian, born about 1885 (married Patrick L. Connolly)

Edward Louis Murphy Jr., born 1888

Ella, born 1890 (married Ibar M. Spellacy)

Generation 3

Edward Louis Murphy Jr., married Frances Tenner in 1912 (she died in 1926)

Their children were: Genevieve, born 1913 (married William G. Maas)

Edward L. Murphy III, born 1915 (married Mercedes M. Shiely)

Dorothie, born 1918 (married A. Gray Fellows)

Althea, born 1920 (married James L. Nelson)

Richard Tenner Murphy, born 1924 (married Helen Duffy)

Edward Murphy Jr., born 1888, married May McGinnis in 1927

Their children were: Carole, born 1929 (married Richard T. Faricy)

Patricia, born 1931 (married George B. Millard)

south of Minneapolis, and planes were flying routes to Rochester, Chicago, and into Wisconsin.

Ironically, new, more flexible, and faster hauling of goods, especially by road and rail, proved to be a boon to the organized crime that tightened its grip on the nation during the thirteen years prohibition was the law of the land. Not just in St. Paul but throughout the country, lawlessness was widespread as a populace unhappy with the 18th Amendment took to concocting home brew anywhere grain, sugar, and yeast could be mixed and fermented in attics, basements, garages, and barns. Bootlegging was so widespread that prohibition violators clogged the nation's courtrooms. Speakeasies nurtured gambling and prostitution. In St. Paul the O'Connor System began to break down.

By the 1930s banks would be robbed, gangsters would shoot it out with law enforcement officers, and prominent businessmen would be kidnapped.

The late 1920s brought tragedy to the Murphy family. On February 10, 1926, a date vividly etched in the memories of her five children, Frances Tenner Murphy died suddenly and unexpectedly in their home on Exeter Place. The family had moved there only three years earlier and the children were enrolled at nearby St. Mark's school. Her daughter Althea remembers turning back to kiss her mother one last time that day before leaving for school. Like his sisters, Frances's son Ed has never forgotten the day of her death.

> My sisters were having lunch at school, but I was heading home for lunch. I came through the St. Thomas College campus and saw Pat Connolly's car and my father's car parked behind the house. I wondered why he was there at midday. When I reached the house, I found that our mother had died sometime that morning after we'd left for school. It was just pandemonium for the next three days.

Frances Murphy had been pregnant with her sixth child. Death was due to a pulmonary embolism with toxemia of pregnancy and thrombophlebitis as a contributory cause. She was thirty-seven years old.

The house at 118 Exeter Place where E. L. Murphy Jr., and his family moved in 1925. Photographed in 2002 by Susan Lightfoot for the Murphy Warehouse Company

THE MURPHYS AND THE CONNOLLYS

Patrick L. Connolly Sr., who married E. L. Murphy's daughter Lillian, was a saloonkeeper like his father-in-law. Owner of a saloon on Jackson Street in downtown St. Paul, Connolly closed it down after the advent of prohibition in 1920, bought some dump trucks, and went into the business of hauling sand and gravel, an operation that became Connolly Contracting Company.

The Connollys, like the Murphys, did well during the 1920s but the Great Depression of the 1930s dealt both families and their companies a devastating blow. Connolly was losing money on the construction of a dam at the Sault Ste. Marie locks in Upper Michigan when American National Bank stepped in. In the words of Connolly's son, Patrick Connolly Jr., "the company by that time was being run by a credit committee that included H. B. Humason." His father didn't live to see the end of the depression and the future prospering of his company. He died in 1934, not long before E. L. Murphy Sr.,'s own death in December of that year.

Of Pat and Lillian Murphy Connolly's three children, Patrick Jr., Joe, and Bart, it was Pat, Jr., who took over the company as president after his father's death. A 1932 graduate of St. Thomas Academy, he had begun work for the company as a dispatcher at the age of eighteen. Connolly Contracting went on to work on the construction of the Fort Peck Dam in Montana

and the Parker Dam in Arizona, among many other projects.

Patrick Connolly Jr., remembered his company's own association with the J. L. Shiely Construction Company: "Joe Shiely suggested that Connolly Contracting be hired to help out with Shiely projects because we had all those dump trucks, so we did. Shiely did the riprap, sand, and gravel. We did the hauling and dumping. Later, in the early 1940s, we got rid of the dump trucks and went into truck transportation. Still later, in 1969, we opened Courier Dispatch, but in 1974 I sold out to a Texas Company and retired."

The Murphy and Connolly association remained lifelong. Patrick Connolly Jr., remembered how he and Ed Murphy "hated Lake Minnewawa" because the lake reminded them of St. Mark's boys camp "and all those mosquito bites." He also remembered how "my father and grandfather—those old controlling Irish guys—hated the banks, probably due to the voting trust and credit committee. Ellen Murphy wore those jewels around her neck because grandfather Murphy didn't believe in banks and was quite vocal about it."

Remembered by her family as deeply religious, Lillian Murphy Connolly became an associate nun after the death of her husband in 1934. Ella Murphy Spellacy, who had four children—Mary, Irene, Babe, and Ibar—outlived her own immediate family. She died in 1991 at the age of 101.

"The wake was held at our house," Ed Murphy remembered. "I think it lasted two days and two nights. In those days, wakes were long. Our house was just loaded with people all the time. My mother was buried from St. Mark's. I remember walking up the aisle with my dad. The church was jammed and people were crying." A small marker beside her grave in Calvary Cemetery reads "Baby Murphy." Frances's sister, Mary Tenner Dickinson, and her husband Fred moved into the Murphy home to care for the children.

Across the street at 2217 Riverwood lived another Irish Catholic family named McGinnis. The family included a son and four daughters, all born in Racine, Wisconsin. "They had a bar in Racine and the family lived upstairs," Carole Faricy said. "It was really Grandmother McGinnis who ran the business. She also did all the cooking for the bar, with a dumb waiter pumping up and down. After the bar fell on hard times, they moved to St. Paul. Their son and a daughter moved on. The other three young women who remained at home all had good jobs; they supported their parents, and they built that house on Riverwood for them."

Months after his wife's death, Murphy began courting May, the youngest of the McGinnis sisters, and on July 29, 1927, they were married, against the wishes of both families who seem to have felt it was "too soon," according to one family member. "But it was a real love affair," Carole Faricy said. "I think that mother was madly in love with my father, and he did love her." They had two children: Carole, who was born in 1929 and would marry architect Richard Faricy in 1961, and Patricia (Patty) Millard, who was born in 1931 and married businessman George Millard in 1955.

May McGinnis Murphy would have an enormous impact on the

Frances Tenner Murphy

Frances Tenner Murphy with one of her daughters, Althea, and one-year-old Dick at 77 Front Street.

fortunes of her husband's company. Thirty-one years old at the time of her marriage, she was an experienced, skilled businesswoman. She had been the personal secretary for Jule Hannaford, president of the Northern Pacific Railway, and, according to Murphy family lore, the first woman to hold that job at a railroad anywhere in the country. "To her dying day she was proud of that," her daughter said. Her friendship with the Hannaford family endured until Hannaford's death.

"I remember going with her to the Hannaford home, which was just off Summit Avenue and across the street from a little park," Dick Murphy said. "It was a big square three-story house. We'd go in, meet him and his wife, and I'd get a lollipop. He called mother 'girl' and she named my sister Carole for his wife."

For a time after May Murphy's marriage, all was well. Dick Murphy remembered how his father set the rules for his two families. "When I was a small boy, my father made it very clear to all of us that we were never to use the terms stepmother, half-brother, or half-sister. He said 'your sisters are your sisters and you are their brothers and that's how we'll run this family.'" His instructions were more than taken to heart. As Carole Faricy remembered it,

Murphy "circus wagons"
in the 1930s

I never knew there were two families until I was in eighth grade. A nun from Derham Hall was visiting St. Mark's and she asked me if I was the product of the first Mrs. Murphy or the second Mrs. Murphy. I ran home from school, got on the phone to the office where both mother and dad were working and yelled, "What's going on here?" That's the only time they both came home at noon. We never discussed it after that, not ever. We didn't talk in those days. I think my brother Richard went for years thinking that he was the baby who killed his mother. My mother adored him. He entered her life when he was at a delightful age. He was only two or three years old, this little boy who'd lost his mother, and I could understand why he was my mother's baby. They had a very close mother-son relationship.

I do remember wondering why everyone called my mother "May dear." Mother told me later that when she came into the family, she didn't want the older children to think she was trying to take their mother's place, so she told them to call her "May dear." Gradually we started sliding into "mother." But when she died, there still were a lot of my friends who never knew she was my father's second wife.

However, Patty Millard remembered that "we did seem to be two families, with Carole as the bridge between them."

May McGinnis joined the Murphy family at a high point in the life of the company. In 1930 the Murphy Transport & Storage Company overcame enormous odds to win permission to operate a motor freight line from the Twin Cities to Duluth. It was the climax of a struggle that involved railroads, other motor freight carriers, and the Duluth Chamber of Commerce. The Murphy company's success, the St. Paul newspapers stated at the time, "is due largely to its three executive heads, E. L. Murphy Sr., president; E. L. Murphy Jr., secretary and St. Paul manager; and Ibar M. Spellacy, vice president and Minneapolis manager; and to the fact that this company is the largest of its kind in the northwest." The elder Murphy, the newspaper noted, started the transfer service twenty years earlier with one team of horses and a wagon:

> Today the transfer company of which he is head operates 200 motor trucks and trailers, 25 teams of horses and has an investment amounting to more than $1,750,000. It serves 200 towns of the northwest with daily store delivery service and it advertises that it can give actual express service at freight rate prices.
>
> It is this concern which petitioned the state railroad and warehouse commission for a certificate of convenience and necessity to operate a motor freight service to Duluth. Despite the opposition of the Duluth Chamber of Commerce, four opposing truck lines and and the four railroads operating to

ears in Trucking Business Bring Prosperity to E. L. Murphy, Jr.

Two Murphys, father and son, from an undated, unidentified newsclipping describing Murphy Transfer & Storage and Murphy Motor Freight Lines before E. L. Murphy Sr.,'s death in 1934.

One of Murphy Rigging and Erecting's early jobs in the 1930s. Murphy Rigging and Erecting was operated by the Murphy Transfer and Storage Company.

Duluth, the Murphy Transfer company was granted the certificate, according to reports of the case given by Mr. Spellacy. Then an order for rehearing was given the petition of the Duluth Chamber of Commerce.

The four railroads and the four bus companies intervened on behalf of the petitioners and again the Murphy [Company] won. The order gives them permission to handle only through freight between the Twin Cities and Duluth.

The Murphy Transfer & Storage Co. recently completed a modern warehouse and truck garage at 9th st. and Broadway where its headquarters are located. It now maintains branches in Duluth, Eau Claire, Faribault, Owatonna, Wabasha, Winona, La Crosse, Jordan, St. Peter, Mankato and Litchfield. The company employs from 250 to 300 men throughout the year,

It was, needless to say, a plum for the Murphys. The fight for the route began in 1928 with the railroads protesting the granting of permits to any of the four competing truck lines, maintaining that the railroads already served the territory adequately. The trucking companies, of course, disagreed; so did the Railroad and Warehouse Commission in announcing that the permit had been granted in response to a "substantial demand" for common carrier truck service between Duluth and the Twin Cities:

> We find and determine that public convenience and necessity requires the establishment of such service. Not to do so would be a discrimination against Duluth and its shippers. Such service, when established, will not authorize the carrier to carry shipments to or from intermediate points.

According to news accounts, three of the trucking companies joining Murphy Transfer & Storage in jockeying for the permit were headquartered in Duluth: Lake Superior Fish & Freight Company, the North Shore Fish & Freight Company, and Sellwood-Johnson Transportation Co. The fourth was the Duluth, St. Paul & Minneapolis

Overland Express in Stillwater. When the Duluth interests combined under the name of Gopher Freight Lines, the fight narrowed to a three-cornered battle among the Stillwater, Duluth, and Twin Cities interests.

Murphy Motor Freight Lines Formed

Edward L. Murphy Jr., displayed for the press the foresight with which the company had planned the operation of a line that at the time was the only one of its kind between the Twin Cities and Duluth. Service could begin immediately, he said. It was to be a nightly run each way, with no intermediate stops. About $50,000 worth of equipment will be used on the line at the start, he said, and within six months $100,000 worth will be in use.

Ibar M. Spellacy about 1928 when he was vice president of Murphy Transfer & Storage Company.

> We plan to use four tractors at first. Two of them with their trailers will leave each end of the line at about 10 P.M. each day and arrive at their destinations early the next morning. As time goes on, this equipment will be added to until we have about eight tractors in operation. . . . The new line will connect in St. Paul with motorized freight lines serving southern Minnesota and in Duluth with lines serving the northern part of the state.

Reflecting the requirements of the new permit, as well as changes in the trucking regulations of 1925 that dictated what a company could carry to certain destinations, Murphy Motor Freight Lines, Inc., was organized on July 1, 1930, as a common motor carrier, an LTL (less-than-truckload) subsidiary of Murphy Transfer & Storage Company. It was, according to the legal documents, incorporated in the state of Delaware " with perpetual existence to do a general motor freight hauling business." Its capital stock "was represented by $4,000 shares of no par common stock and $3,000 shares of 7 percent cumulative preferred stock with a par value of $100 a share." While Murphy Transfer & Storage owned 3,181 shares (75 percent) of Murphy Motor Freight Lines's common stock and 1,495 shares (7 percent) of its preferred stock, the two companies operated as separate corporations under Murphy ownership.

Edward L. Murphy Jr. in 1928.

The future seemed bright, although the New York Stock Market's crash in October 1929 had shaken the country. Many speculators, inured to the surging economy of the 1920s, expected

A "St. Paul Personalities"
sketch from the June 11, 1933
edition of a St. Paul newspaper.
Minnesota Historical Society
newspaper collection.

A "St. Paul Personalities" sketch from the June 11, 1933 edition of a St. Paul newspaper. Minnesota Historical Society newspaper collection.

the market to rally, and it did begin a short-lived recovery. It was not enough, however, to stave off the full fury of a depression that was the worst economic downturn in American history. It was a period of national tragedy that touched bottom in 1931 and remained there for several years. In St. Paul the depression was held at bay for a time. Several major contruction projects, including the First National Bank building and a new St. Paul City Hall-Ramsey County Courthouse, neither of them completed, continued to provide jobs that temporarily fueled the local economy. By 1932, however, homeless men were sleeping on the city's park benches and begging at the back doors in wealthier neighborhoods. Families were torn apart as men left to try to find work elsewhere or to erase the need to feed one more mouth. Some never returned.

Hill Steps In

Tired of what he saw as the ineffectual efforts of the federal government to feed the hungry, Louis W. Hill Sr., suggested that the city's private sector step in and establish a food commissary. When city officials balked, Hill himself, secretly and independently, bought a trainload of food and stored the food in caves on Eagle Street below Seven Corners. Potatoes, rutabagas, rice, and other vegetables were divided into food packages and distributed to needy families.

As the depression deepened, the Murphys watched their costs. Since tires were a major expense for the two companies, in 1932 E. L. Murphy turned to the Goodyear Tire Company for an evaluation of the Tire Operating Conditions on the fleet of trucks maintained by both Murphy Transfer & Storage and Murphy Motor Freight Lines. The Goodyear report is a careful description of Murphy Transfer & Storage Company and Murphy Motor Freight Lines as they were in the early 1930s The report noted that the Transfer Company "was one of the oldest and largest operations of its kind in the Twin Cities," that it was engaged in freight transfer among the various railroad terminals in St. Paul and Minneapolis, and that the fleet was generally used in pickup deliveries as well as contract hauling for such accounts as

THE EFFECT OF THE GREAT DEPRESSION IN ST. PAUL

The late A. A. Heckman, who arrived in St. Paul in 1931 to direct the work of United Charities (now Family Service of St. Paul), remembered the Great Depression vividly. From his office in the now-demolished Wilder Building, he watched men pacing up and down on the sidewalk outside, trying to make up their minds to come in and apply for relief.

"Welfare," he recalled, "either private or public, was a shameful thing for family men who, all their adult lives, had had jobs, had been self-supporting, had been good citizens who had contributed to a church and to other community needs. All of a sudden there was no money in their pockets and it was a drastic, shocking, demoralizing situation."

As the depression wore on, he was asked to set up a public welfare program for Ramsey County.

He remembered a "moat," actually a recessed sidewalk, that surrounded the old Ramsey County Courthouse between Wabasha and Cedar Avenues where the county welfare board had its office.

"I remember very well seeing that 'moat' filled with people. They stood four abreast in a line that ran all around the courthouse and extended along Wabasha for at least two blocks. . . . We had more than one woman on a high stool passing out vouchers. We had quite a number of trained workers who just could not seem to work fast enough to take care of all the people who were waiting for the large and small grocery vouchers—the $5 or $10 grocery orders. An order for a small family was supposed to last that family for a month, but it often ran out before the month ended and they would have to find other means to put food on their tables."

A Murphy truck with the National Biscuit Company identification logo in 1930s. National Biscuit's predecessor was Murphy Transfer's first account, dating back to 1908, and Murphy Trucking was still hauling for the company thirty years later.

the Winston-Newell Grocery Company, Gamble & Robinson, E. P. Stacy, Sears, Roebuck, Montgomery Ward, and A & P. Murphy Motor Freight Lines, the report explained, was "owned and controlled" by Murphy Transfer & Storage, the parent company, and "engaged primarily in distance hauling" between Twin Cities warehouses and terminals and in making daily trips to out-state cities. By 1932 its network also included Mankato and Albert Lea in Minnesota; Chippewa Falls and Eau Claire in Wisconsin, and Mason City in Iowa.

The report was exhaustive. It covered not just tire service and operating conditions and the advantages of balloon tires, but such other essentials as alignment of tires (they should be systematically checked) and the importance of a driver's attitude. ("A careless driver can cause more damage than can be offset by all other factors combined.")

The depression was a disaster for the Murphys. Embedded within it were the seeds of a tragic loss and a bitter family upheaval, an unforgettable episode that would change the course of history for the family and the company. Although by 1933 Murphy Transfer & Storage Company, according to the *St. Paul News*, had "250 pieces of equipment such as trucks and tractors, two storage houses, and serves [customers] in Minnesota, Iowa & Wisconsin daily," business was dropping precipitously and billings to customers went unpaid. The Murphys feared an additional level of regulation when the new federal Interstate Commerce Commission assumed jurisdiction over all carriers in 1935. Besides that, there was the $220,000 indebtedness the company had incurred in building the Minneapolis and St. Paul warehouses. American National Bank was calling for payment and refusing to put any more money into the company.

The bank apparently was worried, too, and for good reason. During the 1920s the failures among Twin Cities banks had become terrifyingly frequent. American Bank, with Harry B. Humason as vice

The 'Bremer Bank'

The American National Bank, where the Murphys maintained their business account until 1936, was known informally as the "Bremer Bank" because of its close association with the Bremer brothers, Otto the banker and Adolf the brewer. American National Bank was established in 1903 as a result of a long line of bank mergers that dated back to 1882 when the People's Bank of St. Paul was organized. After its dissolution in 1895, the Northern Exchange Bank was formed; Northern Exchange became the American Exchange Bank in 1899.

Four years later the American National Bank was created out of a merger of the American Exchange Bank with the Union Bank. Both banks had barely managed to survive the 1890s, a decade of financial panics that had taught bankers considerable respect for solvency and liquidity.

The scene was set for the emergence in the banking community of the Bremer brothers who had emigrated from Germany in 1867. Otto, who had worked for a bank back in Germany, was serving the first of five terms as St. Paul city treasurer. He became a charter member of Ameri-

can's first board of directors and a minor stockholder. Accumulating shares as the years wore on, he was by 1924 the bank's major shareholder and chairman of its board.

Adolf, an experienced brewmaster in his native Germany, had taken over operating control of his father-in-law's Jacob Schmidt Brewing Company, and Otto joined the brewery as secretary/treasurer. It was a close and mutually supportive relationship, with Adolf often loaning Otto money to invest in the bank.

About the same time, Harry B. Humason, who would play such a major role in the Murphys' business affairs, was working his way up through the ranks at the bank. He became vice president in 1929 and president in 1939. The Murphys, father and son, had known the Bremers and Humason long and well. The onset of the agricultural depression of the 1920s, however, combined with prohibition, dealt both bank and brewery heavy blows. Both bank and brewery survived, but the brewery halted its production of beer. The voting trust that transferred control of Murphy Transport & Storage Company to the bank was a product of that troubled era.

president, demanded that a voting trust be set up to handle the financial affairs of the Murphy Transfer & Storage Company. This would take management of the company out of the hands of its officers, the two Murphys and Spellacy. (A voting trust is a normal instrument for banks to use when they want control of a company. It requires a company's stockholders to surrender their stock to the trust. As long as an indebtedness exists, all decisions need bank approval. Because the Murphy Transfer & Storage Company was in debt to the bank, the bank wanted the right to vote its stock.)

In the midst of this dire period in the depths of the depression, at a special stockholders' meeting on March 6, 1934, Edward L. Murphy Sr., resigned as president and treasurer of Murphy Transfer & Storage Company and Murphy Motor Freight Lines. Family members believe that he was forced out, perhaps by the bank, in a move to take over the faltering company. Spellacy succeeded him as president and Edward L. Murphy Jr., stepped into Spellacy's former post as vice president.

The Truck Drivers Strike

That summer the company was embroiled in new turmoil. A virtual civil war, the Truck Drivers Strike of 1934 broke out on the streets of downtown Minneapolis. It was a desperate depression-era struggle by members of Local 574 of the International Brotherhood of Teamsters for unionization, a closed shop, wage increases, and shorter hours. In May, when two businessmen acting as special deputies were killed during fighting in the Minneapolis warehouse district, Governor Floyd B. Olson authorized the calling of 2,500 Minnesota National Guardsmen in an effort to restore peace, if violence were to erupt again.

The St. Paul truckers voted to strike, although they belonged to a different union, but accepted arbitration instead. However, the Murphy truckers inevitably were entangled in the violence in Minneapolis. Edward L. Murphy Jr., joined the Citizens' Alliance, a group of Minneapolis employers formed to oppose the strikers. "My father told stories of being on that negotiating committee, and of being out on the streets in the midst of the strike," Dick Murphy remembered.

A truce in May proved to be temporary when fighting broke out again in July. On July 20, "Bloody Friday," the Minneapolis police under the command of Chief Mike Johannes fired on a group of

A "Rube Goldberg"-looking 1920s self-propelled concrete mixer hauled by Murphy Transport & Storage Company.

unarmed strikers who were trying to prevent the police from moving a truck. Two strikers were killed and sixty-seven persons were wounded, including thirteen bystanders. Governor Olson subsequently appealed to President Roosevelt to use the Reconstruction Finance Corporation to force a settlement by the employers, and Roosevelt did intervene. Olson, however, had earlier in July declared martial law, a move bitterly denounced by both sides. No parking was allowed in downtown Minneapolis; no liquor was served after 9 P.M.; dance halls and night clubs were closed down at midnight; no picketing of trucks was allowed; and no trucks could move without the military permits that went only to those hauling fruit, milk, and other food. Dick Murphy recalled that,

> Our trucks handled a lot of foodstuffs for the grocery stores. Wire fencing was welded over the windshields and the side windows; then the trucks were sent out with men on them armed with clubs for protection, Several of those trucks were attacked and damaged, and one of them was stopped in

E. L. MURPHY RITES TO BE HELD FRIDAY

Active and Honorary Pallbearers Named for Transfer Firm Founder.

Funeral services for E. L. Murphy of St. Paul, founder of the Murphy Transfer Co., who died in the home of a daughter in Minneapolis Wednesday, will be held in the Catholic Church of the Nativity, Prior and Stanford avenues, at 9 A. M. Friday. Burial will be in Calvary cemetery.

From 1 P. M. today until 8:30 A. M. Friday the body will be in the home of a son, E. L. Murphy Jr., 118 Exeter place, St. Paul.

The elder Mr. Murphy died from injuries suffered in an automobile accident September 6.

Honorary pallbearers will be Otto Bremer, Adolph Bremer, Judge J. C. Michael, E. A. Young, Henry McColl and L. E. Shepley, all of St. Paul; Colonel W. F. Henry and Fred Kaiser, both of Duluth; Samuel B. Wilson of Mankato, former chief justice of the Minnesota State Supreme court; Ivan Bowen, Frank McCormick and Frank Mulcahey, all of Minneapolis.

Fred Saam, Mark Rogers, Lee Sutton, Thomas Walsh and Robert Peters, all of St. Paul, and Harry Jones of Minneapolis, will be active pallbearers.

Survivors are the widow, two daughters and his son and a brother. The daughters are: Mrs. Ibar M. Spellacy, in whose home he died, and Mrs. Patrick L. Connolly, also of Minneapolis. The brother, John J. Murphy, lives in Duluth. Twelve grandchildren also survive.

Edward L. Murphy Sr.'s, obituary in the December 13, 1934, issue of the St. Paul Pioneer Press. *Minnesota Historical Society newspaper collection. (Some sources state that his brother had died earlier.)*

downtown Minneapolis by a mob of strikers. They dragged the driver out, beat him up, took the truck, and ran it into the river near Hennepin Avenue. It was a single-unit truck, not a tractor-trailer.

Ultimately, the strike produced modest gains for the workers. Gradually, over a longer term, Minneapolis lost its anti-union coloration and Local 574 became a power nationally in over-the-road trucking.

Five months after the end of the strike, E. L. Murphy Sr., died on December 12, 1934, at the age of seventy-two. Earlier, on September 6, he had been severely injured in an automobile accident at Kison, Iowa, while on his way to California. He suffered a concussion fracture of the ribs and tibia, and he never fully recovered. His wife Ellen was unable to care for him and they spent the last months of his life at the Minneapolis homes of their daughters, Lillian Connolly and Ella Spellacy, and there he died at Ella's house at 3400 West Calhoun Boulevard. Cause of death, as stated on his death certificate, was "broncho pneumonia" of five-days duration, with "arterio sclerosis" of three-years duration as a contributing cause. His son, in filling out his death certificate, listed his father's occupation as owner of a transfer business, and stated that the last date he had worked at this occupation was June 30, 1927. Even so, he had continued to hold his title as president and treasurer of Murphy Transfer & Storage and Murphy Motor Freight Lines and he was credited with a major role in negotiating the permit to establish the Twin Cities-Duluth truck line in 1930.

A dominating man, he was a force in the business and political life of the Twin Cities, as well as within his family. Family stories maintain that because E. L. Murphy Sr., provided the money and the connections, he called the shots throughout his lifetime, but it was his son who actually ran the company. As Ed Murphy said, "My grandfather was in trucking and real estate, but in true Irish fashion, politics held his heart. He enjoyed it more than he did business."

His grandchildren remember him as a formidable person. His relationship with his older grandchildren seems to have been close and affectionate, but Carole Faricy, who was five years old when he died, recalls "visiting him only once or twice and I don't remember grandpa speaking to me or me to him." She does remember his wake, which was held at her family's home on Exeter Place. "It lasted a long time. He was laid out in the sunroom of the house, right under where Patty and I slept, and I had nightmares about that. I don't remember him standing up. Only lying down." Patty Millard saw him as "a very difficult man, a powerful man."

His death blew the lid off a simmering battle for control of the company and the passage of time has done little to dilute the embittered memories and the sense of betrayal over what happened next. Conflicting stories, interpretations, and perceptions have clouded memories of the events of 1935. One account is from Ed Murphy:

> After grandfather died, it developed that in his will he had made provision that his 164 shares of stock in Murphy Transfer Company would go to Ibar Spellacy, his son-in-law, and not to my father, his son. That caused tremendous problems. Those 164 shares meant that Spellacy now held the controlling block of stock in the company.

Dick Murphy tells a slightly different story but with the same essentials:

> A family battle erupted after my grandfather died and it became known that grandpa had transferred stock, unbeknownst to my father, to his son-in-law and daughter, the Spellacys, giving them 51 percent of the control of the company. We don't know why he did this. My father always

One of the Murphys' Mack trucks hauling an underground fuel tank, perhaps for the gas company. Those tires are solid rubber.

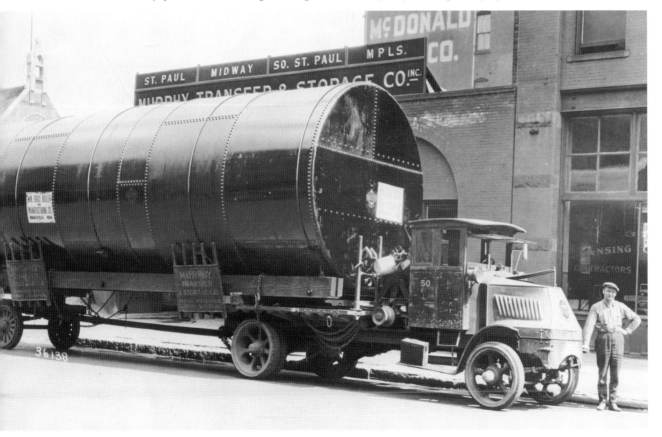

maintained that grandpa's mind was not right. My father told me, "I know he loved me. I was his son. I was the one who was supposed to take over." But Ibar was a good salesman, he was a son-in-law and I suppose grandpa had to give him a job.

My father's fear of banks, actually hatred of banks, came because of the treatment he received after grandpa died and he suddenly found that control of the company was in the hands of Ibar and the American National Bank of St Paul. Here my father was the son, representing the blood line. The bank backed Ibar, not my father, and the bank and Ibar just literally threw my father out. Ibar worked with H. B. Humason, who was vice president of the bank. He and Ibar were buddies, I guess, and they just made life miserable for my father, according to what he told me.

There are other threads to this sad story. One is that in the depths of despair over the future of the company as the depression hit bottom, E. L. Murphy Sr., remarked to Harry Humason that he thought Spellacy "was better qualified to run the business" than was his son, and the bank followed that course. Another, according to Carole Faricy, is that "my mother said grandpa left the business to Spellacy because he thought dad was a better salesman than businessman." And Patty Millard has said that "I have a strong feeling my father would never have lived up to what his father expected of him." Perhaps it was simply that well-known in-bred hostility of father toward heir that has surfaced in other families, particularly those headed by an entrepreneur who also was founder of a family enterprise.

Family accounts, however, are at variance with the few records that remain accessible at this late date. In his will, dated June 29, 1934, Edward L. Murphy Sr., left all his property to his wife, naming her executor of his estate. He made no mention of Ibar Spellacy, the company, or Spellacy's stock in the company, nor did he make any provision for his children, "believing that in the event that my said wife survives me that she will make suitable provision for the said children."

Another record concerns the senior Murphy's 164 shares of Murphy Transfer Company stock. The company's stock book records Murphy's surrender of those shares to Humason for assignment to the voting trust. The transfer is dated February 20, 1935, the date the shares of the other stockholders also were transferred into the voting trust. Although E. L. Murphy Sr. had died two months earlier, it would seem that he already had agreed to transfer his stock, not to Spellacy but to the voting trust.

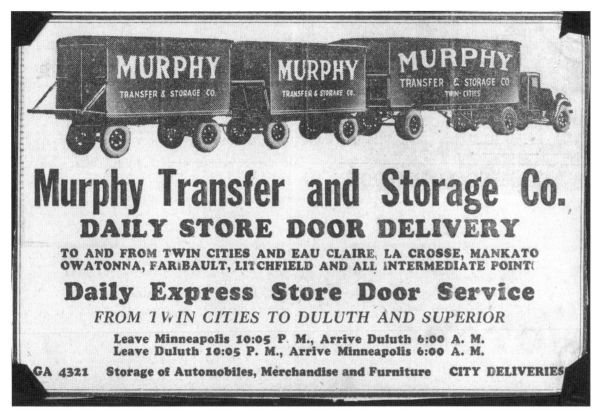

Murphy Transfer and Storage Co.
DAILY STORE DOOR DELIVERY
TO AND FROM TWIN CITIES AND EAU CLAIRE, LA CROSSE, MANKATO
OWATONNA, FARIBAULT, LITCHFIELD AND ALL INTERMEDIATE POINT
Daily Express Store Door Service
FROM TWIN CITIES TO DULUTH AND SUPERIOR
Leave Minneapolis 10:05 P. M., Arrive Duluth 6:00 A. M.
Leave Duluth 10:05 P. M., Arrive Minneapolis 6:00 A. M.
GA 4321   Storage of Automobiles, Merchandise and Furniture   CITY DELIVERIES

*Murphy "circus wagons"
in an ad from the 1934
St. Paul City Directory.*

E. L. Murphy Trucking Emerges

Whatever happened, the result remains clear: Control of the Murphy
Transfer & Storage Company and Murphy Motor Freight Lines had
slipped from Murphy hands. A special stockholders' meeting held on
February 18, 1935, to fill the vacancy caused by the elder Murphy's
death signaled the transfer of power over the affairs of the company
to the voting trust. Ibar Spellacy moved into the presidency; Edward L. Murphy Jr., (who now would be known as Edward L. Murphy
Sr.,) became vice president; and Joseph A. Lethert, an American Bank
officer, was elected to fill the elder Murphy's position on the board. A
new position, assistant to the president (Spellacy) and comptroller,
was created and filled by C. Brewer Goodsell, also an American Bank
officer.

Another important bit of business was transacted at that special
meeting on February 18, 1935. The minutes recorded it: "Officers
agreed to borrow $15,000 from Ellen Murphy in return for a promis-
sory note." And an enduring family mystery ensued. Where did the
money come from? It was unusual then for a woman to have much
money of her own, and $15,000 at that time was a great deal of money.
Carole Faricy has offered one clue. She remembered that when she

was a child, her grandmother Murphy had loose diamonds in a little chamois bag that she wore around her neck.

> We used to look at those diamonds and think they were wonderful. I don't know what happened to all of them. My mother once said that the $15,000 loan helped start the E. L. Murphy Trucking Company in 1936. Perhaps grandmother sold some of them, but I vividly remember those diamonds in that little pouch.

Dick Murphy has offered another clue:

> My grandfather and father were doing very well in the trucking business, but during the 1920s my father and other businessmen had developed that deep-seated distrust of banks. Whenever my grandfather or father had some extra money, they sometimes would pass it along to grandmother and probably some other family members. It wasn't always in cash.

Drawing from an unidentified St. Paul newspaper around 1925.

56

> Sometimes they put it into jewelry, and those jewels might
> have been what grandmother wore in that little chamois
> pouch around her neck. They were mostly diamonds, I think.

Did Ellen Murphy sell some of her diamonds to raise that $15,000? Perhaps it came from her husband's estate, of which she was executor. Whatever its source, Ellen Murphy's loan became a bargaining chip in the rancorous, long-drawn-out fight over the company.

It is difficult to untangle, at this far remove, the maneuverings, and the manipulations that placed Spellacy and the voting trust in control of Murphy Transfer & Storage Company and Murphy Motor Freight Lines. The furious question at first was how could such a take-over be defeated? Was E. L. Murphy of sound mind? Could this be challenged in court? Was he under undue influence from Spellacy family members, who always had been close to him? There were threats and counter-threats, there were questions about ownership of the Transfer Company stock that went into the voting trust, even though the stock certificates themselves clearly record the other transfers on February 20, 1935: 125 shares from Edward L. Murphy (now Sr.); 10 shares from Ibar Spellacy; one share from Ellen Murphy.

Throughout the bitter struggle, the second E. L. Murphy had retained ownership of his stock. After 1935, when his shares went into the voting trust, he found however that his role in the company was gradually diminishing and he was soon reduced to that of employee. In short, according to the family, he was being pushed out of the business.

Worse was to come, and it arrived not long after a happy family event, the marriage at St. Mark's Church on August 10, 1936, of his oldest child, Genevieve, to banker William G. Maas. Carole Faricy remembered the wedding and its aftermath:

> Gen had a huge wedding with lots of attendants. They had a
> wedding breakfast at the Town and Country Club with hun-
> dreds of people there. Bill Maas was from a prominent fam-
> ily. Then they all came back to our house for a big reception.
> In those days, they used to have what they called a jamboree
> when all the kids in the neighborhood would come and throw
> coins at the couple. Patty and I were wearing little Dutch hats
> and I remember my father patting me on the back and saying,
> "Get out there and get some of that cash." Money must have
> been tight.

Several days later, her brother Dick opened the front door. There stood a process server with an eviction notice ordering the family to vacate the house within forty-eight hours. For Carole Faricy, at the age of seven, "it was just so exciting."

> I remember my brother driving the car with my mother and going place-to-place trying to find a house to rent. She didn't have any credit. At about 7 o'clock at night she rang the doorbell at Fred McCarthy's house on Summit Avenue. She talked to Fred, then got back in the car and said we had a place to live. It was a small house at 1891 Ashland Avenue. Because we had the trucks, we were all loading them up. We had to get out of 118 Exeter, pronto.

Two months later E. L. Murphy submitted a terse notice, dated October 5, 1936: "To the Shareholders of Murphy Transfer & Storage Company: Gentlemen: The undersigned resigns as a Director of your corporation, the resignation to be effective upon acceptance. Yours truly, E. L. Murphy." In a similarly worded notice bearing the same date, he also resigned as "Vice President of Murphy Transfer & Storage Company." The company's board of directors accepted his resignations and elected Goodsell to succeed him as vice president at a special meeting held October 12 at the Endicott Building in downtown St. Paul.

In exchange for his resignation, Murphy hammered out a settlement with the voting trust. Half of the 164 shares of stock his father had owned would go to him, and half to Spellacy. There remained the $15,000 Ellen Murphy had loaned Murphy Transfer & Storage Company during its darkest days. It was a debt the company, under the management of Spellacy and the voting trust, was unable or unwilling to pay. Murphy now played his card.

"Sell me some of the Murphy Transfer & Storage Company assets," he said in effect, "and I will release the $15,000 so the bank won't have to pay it." Actually, he traded the note for some of the Transfer company's "old iron," that would help him make a new start. In the typically measured words of a legal agreement, the minutes of October 16, 1936, recorded the shareholders' decision:

> WHEREAS, the shareholders of this corporation by an instrument in writing [authorize] the officers of this corporation to sell to Edward L. Murphy the following described personal property, together with the unused portions of the 1936 licenses covering the tractors, trucks and trailers hereafter described and issued by the State of Minnesota, to wit:

A list of "the following described personal property" included nine tractors, twenty-three trucks, twenty-six trailers, and a Ford sedan, together

A newspaper ad from around 1935 after management of Murphy Transfer & Storage and Murphy Motor Freight Lines passed to I. M. Spellacy and American National Bank's voting trust. Minnesota Historical Society newspaper collection.

with their batteries and spare parts and "all blocks, timbers, rollers, pinch-bars, simple jacks, snatch blocks, chains and binders, chain blocks ropes, hand windlass, and one half of the furniture pads." In addition, Murphy acquired an Underwood typewriter, two desks, four chairs, a four-drawer metal filing cabinet, and a metal wastebasket.

The minutes further stated that $15,000 of the equipment's total cost of $20,000 was "to be paid for by the delivery for cancellation of that certain promissory note executed and delivered by the Murphy Transfer & Storage Company to one Ellen Murphy, together with satisfaction of the mortgage executed and delivered to said Ellen Murphy to secure said note with the understanding that said Edward L. Murphy shall furnish to said Ellen Murphy independent consideration inuring to her for the surrender of said note and mortgage."

Through it all, although the bank was voting his stock, E. L. Murphy remained a stockholder in Murphy Transfer & Storage and Murphy Motor Freight Lines. Their minutes would record his presence or that of his son at stockholders meetings, always identified as "holder of a Trustee's Certificate."

On October 8, 1936 Murphy struck out on his own with a new company that would be known as the E. L. Murphy Trucking Company. It would concentrate initially on warehousing and local and specialized hauling of freight in the Twin Cities area. Murphy Motor Freight Lines, under the management of Spellacy and the bank, went its own way, focusing on "over-the-road" hauling, and becoming the "big ship" of its parent company, Murphy Transfer & Storage. Not surprisingly, and despite his fear of banks, Murphy moved his bank account from American to First National Bank. It would remain an enduring relationship and his son, Ed Murphy, would in years to come serve on the bank's board. In the meantime, the elder Murphy had almost no cash. The depression had not loosened its grip; nobody seemed to have any money, except, as it turned out, his son.

"I had started my second year of law school at the University, registered and paid my tuition that September of 1936, when it became necessary to join my father in the new company," Ed Murphy recalled. "I went back to the University and they refunded the $75 I'd paid for my tuition. That became the cash with which we started E. L. Murphy Trucking Company. We were careful what name we used so it wouldn't be confused with the company the bank now controlled."

It had required enormous courage for Murphy to start over in the midst of the frightening depression and the unknowns created by the federal Motor Carrier Act of 1935, perhaps until 1980 the single most important legislation aimed at regulating the trucking industry. Placed under the jurisdiction of the Interstate Commerce Commission (the ICC), the Act's requirements created a far more complicated work environment for many company owners, but many also welcomed that protection. Common carriers were required to apply for

Straight truck and trailer, 1930s—red top, gold letters, yellow bottom.

a Certificate of Public Convenience and Necessity which spelled out the types of freight to be hauled and routes to be used. Uniform rates were stabilized, maximum hours established, standard accounting methods set, and competition brought under control. Shippers could depend on regular service. With its multiple requirements, the Act tended to favor the larger, well-established firms and weed out the smaller, less stable operations—a matter of considerable importance in that depression-induced free-wheeling period.

'I Ran a Railroad'

At the newly established E. L. Murphy Trucking Company, May Murphy, with two small children of her own and responsibilities for others from her husband's first family, stepped in to help. There is a family story that when someone asked her, "What makes you think you can run a trucking company?" she responded, "Why not? I ran a railroad." It made sense. During her years with the Northern Pacific, all railroads did an immense amount of business with trucking companies, despite competing with them at the same time. Carole Faricy remembered how her mother managed both home and office:

Norman Kittson's racing stable at 1350 University Avenue. Once the Bohn Refrigerator Company's building, this also was the headquarters for Murphy Motor Freight Lines and (briefly) for E. L. Murphy Trucking in 1936, the year this photograph was taken. The building was demolished in 1942. Photo by A. F. Raymond, Minnesota Historical Society archives.

Norman W. Kittson, ca. 1865. fur trader, entrepreneur, real estate investor, he also was a pioneer in the business of carting and hauling with his Red River ox carts. Some seventy years later, a Murphy Warehouse was built on Kittson's Addition in downtown St. Paul. Minnesota Historical Society photograph.

While we were still living at 118 Exeter we had a wonderful woman, Esther, who lived with us in the house, so we had help all the time and mother didn't have to worry too much about running the household. Still, I don't know how she did it. She worked until late; then she came home, supervised the dinner and took care of us. I remember doing the washing in the basement. We had those old wringers and Dick and I would be down there with soap all over the place and laundry hanging up. Most of those people in that little ghetto on Exeter had someone living with them who was from the country and was just like family.

The Murphys set up a tiny office, an upstairs room in an old building at 1350 University Avenue, a neighborhood known as Kittsondale. Once pioneer fur trader Norman Kittson's million-dollar racing stable, the building now was owned by the Bohn Refrigerator Company. Facilities for the newly launched E. L. Murphy Trucking company were spartan, to say the least. A single light bulb hung from the ceiling. There was the desk, chair, metal wastebasket, and the old typewriter Murphy had acquired as part of his agreement with the voting trust, and there was a telephone. Murphy Transfer & Storage and Murphy Motor Freight Lines had their headquarters in the same building and remained there through the 1930s. Ed Murphy remembered that "The freight lines let us stay there until we found somewhere else to go."

It was a good location at the time because it was between the two cities. Within the year, however, we moved to Minneapolis and rented part of a building across the street from some old streetcar barns on the north side of the Mississippi, not too far from the Great Northern Railroad station. In 1937 we moved back to St. Paul, to 1924 University Avenue, and we stayed there for the next thirty years.

That the company could follow a gradual but determined ascent into new but hard-won prosperity was due in part to E. L. Murphy's ability and drive as a salesman and to May Murphy's management skills. She typed out checks and bills and answered the phone. When payment was slow, she would put on her hat and her white gloves and, sometimes with a child in tow, she would pay personal calls on debtors. When a debtor balked, she was known to sit in his office until he paid.

The company, in its early years, was basically a machinery moving and local cartage business. E. L. Murphy maintained a long-standing agreement, dating back to his father's day, to haul groceries, including the famous yellow label Home Brand foods for Griggs Cooper & Company, the largest wholesale grocery house west of Chicago. Murphy still had the contract, dating back to 1927, to store and haul the

WHO WAS NORMAN KITTSON?

Norman Wolfred Kittson, fur trader and business partner of James J. Hill and Henry Hastings Sibley, was a pioneer in the carting and hauling business that E. L. Murphy Sr., would enter some sixty years later. Kittson was born near Sorel, in what was then known as Lower Canada, on March 5, 1814. His grandfather had served under the British general, James Wolfe, at Quebec and his grandmother later married the renowned explorer Alexander Henry.

In 1830, when Kittson was sixteen, he joined the American Fur Company and headed to Mackinac Island, the great center of America's fur trade in the North. There he met Sibley and the friendship and the business they forged together was to last the rest of their lives. In 1843 Sibley, now based at Mendota as the fur company's chief agent, and Kittson formed a partnership, with Kittson in charge of fur posts strung along the western and northern boundaries of what is now Minnesota. Based in Pembina in today's North Dakota, Kittson adapted the carts used by the Indians for their buffalo hunts and the Red River ox cart was born. For almost another twenty years, the carts would

haul furs from Kittson's trading posts to St. Paul where they would be shipped east.

By 1855 Kittson had settled in St. Paul. He bought real estate, known as Kittson's Addition, that included much of downtown St. Paul. He was elected St. Paul's mayor in 1858. Two years later, as manager of a line of inland steamboats, he met James J. Hill and the two established the Red River Transportation Company. He also was associated with Hill in forming what became the Great Northern Railway. By 1882 Kittson had built the Globe office building in downtown St. Paul, the Astoria Hotel, a $40,000 addition to the Clarendon Hotel, and a huge mansion on the site of the present St. Paul Cathedral.

His business life eclipsed his personal life. He was known to have had two—possibly four— Indian wives before marrying Mary A. Kittson, who was from Fort Garry, near Winnipeg, Canada. They had five children, but his will lists eleven, and a geneology developed by a grandson suggests twenty-six. Family records indicate that Kittson provided for all of his children. He died May 11, 1888, somewhere between Chicago and St. Paul, on his way home from a trip.

KITTSONDALE AND THE MURPHYS

Kittsondale, where E. L. Murphy Trucking Company opened its first office in 1936 and Murphy Motor Freight had its own offices throughout the 1930s, was Norman Kittson's pride and joy. Located at about the present-day intersection of Snelling and University Avenues, this was a million-dollar stable and driving park (horse track) built by the fur trader, transportation pioneer, and real estate millionaire. The stables alone cost $60,000. Laid out in the form of a Greek cross, they measured 248 by 180 feet and housed sixty-four box stalls.

Kittson also owned Erdheim, a world-famous horse farm outside Philadelphia. "Iroquoise," the first American horse to win the British Derby, was raised and trained there. Although the expanding commerce of the Midway District eventually swallowed up the race track itself, the Kittsondale stables were not torn down until 1942.

cases for Sears, Roebuck's refrigerators. The cases for the Sears referigerators were built in St. Paul by the Seeger Refrigerator company in its plant on Arcade Street.

"We had empty freighthouse buildings and we found space in other buildings where we stored the cases," Dick Murphy said. "Forklifts hadn't been invented, so the men had to do what we referred to as 'bull work'—unload the cases with a two-wheel truck, take them down a ramp, then over to where they could be stored."

Murphy Trucking continued to do all the installation work for Diebold Safe and Lock Company, an account dating back to the early years of Murphy Transfer Company. Diebold sold bank equipment, vault doors, and safe-deposit boxes throughout the Upper Midwest, and E. L. Murphy was a good friend, a bridge and golfing partner, of Diebold's district manager.

"It was with the support of the Diebold company," Dick Murphy recalled, " that my father got the first piece of interstate authority for E. L. Murphy Trucking Company. Another piece of interstate authority came later and that had to do with serving the Twin Cities area as a cartage company, occasionally going out-of-town into the five-state area of the Dakotas, Iowa, Minnesota, and Wisconsin."

Murphy worked hard at building and maintaining his many friendships among his fellow businessmen. Some of those friendships were nurtured through golf or bridge at the Town and Country Club; some at meetings at the Ryan Hotel in downtown St. Paul; some at evenings at Napoleon's, later known as the Criterion, a well-known University Avenue restaurant that was a favorite gathering spot for politicians and for the businessmen whose offices spread along University or out into the warehouse district to the north and west.

"They were all buddies there, groups of buddies, contemporaries," Patty Millard said. "They played together and drank together. It was a fairly small community of men. Everybody was working with everybody else and competing with each other."

Murphy also worked hard at maintaining his political connections, and he watched legislative sessions closely, particularly the debates over the fallout following passage of the Interstate Commerce Act in 1935. He once told his son that "nothing happens at the legislature between eight and five in the afternoon, only at 5 o'clock in the morning."

E. L. Murphy Trucking Company office at 1924 University Avenue in 1937.
Photo by Kenneth M. Wright Studios, Minnesota Historical Society collections.

He was "absolutely crushed," Ed Murphy recalled, "when the legislature passed the first regulatory act back in 1925. That meant we couldn't do what we were doing without a certificate. Well, we were first in line, we got certificates to do that particular type of cartage, and it all turned out to be a blessing in disguise for trucking companies like ours."

Ed Murphy returned to the University of Minnesota to complete his law degree, then to practice law with the Minneapolis firm known at the time as Stinchfield Mackall Crounse and Moore. Other family members pitched in to help. Gradually, Murphy built an extensive fleet of motor vehicles that operated up and down University Avenue

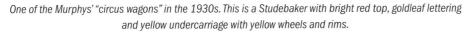

One of the Murphys' "circus wagons" in the 1930s. This is a Studebaker with bright red top, goldleaf lettering and yellow undercarriage with yellow wheels and rims.

between the warehouses and the adjacent rail areas in Minneapolis and St. Paul.

* * *

Carole Faricy remembered the last years of the 1930s as among the happiest years of her life:

> I loved those years we lived at 1891 Ashland. They were wonderful years. All of us were together. The kitchen was small. In order to eat, we had to turn the dining room table sideways. I remember that the dining room was blue and the living room had pink wallpaper. I thought that was the neatest thing in the world. We had three bedrooms upstairs. My sisters and I had the biggest bedroom, which wasn't really that big. Mother and dad were across the hall, my brothers in the third bedroom. We had one closet in our room, but we went to St. Mark's and wore school uniforms so we didn't have a lot of clothes. And we had one bathroom. You know, everyone was so modest in those days. Everyone was up in the morning. How we ever got in and out I don't know. Eight of us and one bathroom. Mother called the house her "love nest."

She remembered that her older sister, called Dorie within the family, was still living at home and she "took over the household. Mother went to work and Dorie ran the house, even though at the same time

A line-up of Mack and White trucks at the Murphys' at Ninth and Broadway in St. Paul's Lowertown.

she was working at the Golden Rule department store in downtown St. Paul. If she thought she'd be late getting home at night, she'd lock the doors before she left in the morning. We'd have to sit outside and wait for her. She didn't want us running through the house, messing it up. But we all loved her. Dorie was our mother and she was a wonderful disciplinarian."

They were still at 1891 Ashland in 1940 when Ed Murphy married Mercedes Shiely, uniting two well-known Irish Catholic families. She was the granddaughter of Joseph L. Shiely Sr., whose teamsters had hauled the stone to the new state Capitol in the early 1900s.

"That's an argument I remember mother and dad having," Carole Faricy said. "Mother wanted to have the bridal dinner at the St. Paul Athletic Club because our house was so small, but Ed insisted on having it at home. So we had the bridal dinner at home." The family didn't remain there long, however. In the early 1940s they moved to 2020 Portland Avenue, which would remain the family home for almost twenty more years.

On December 7, 1941, E. L. Murphy Sr., had a serious heart attack. "I heard about Pearl Harbor when I was in the car with my siblings following the ambulance to the hospital," Dick Murphy remembered. "My brother and my mother were in the car ahead of us. Dad was ill for some time. Mother was still working at the company as sort of an overseer, holding it all together, although we also had some administrative

The small house at 1891 Ashland Avenue where the Murphy family moved in 1936.
Photographed in 2002 by Susan Lightfoot for the Murphy Warehouse Company

help." Ed Murphy left the practice of law to join his father once again
in the trucking company.

A year later Dick Murphy graduated from St. Thomas Academy on
June 4, 1942, his eighteenth birthday. Because of his military training
there, he was commissioned a second lieutenant in the United States
army, sent off to Camp Wolter, Texas, and assigned to an infantry
replacement-training unit. Returning home, he entered the University of Minnesota where he graduated in 1946. Intending to complete
a law degree, he instead responded to his family's needs and went to
work to help his father at E.L. Murphy Trucking Company. Events had
begun to move fast for the Murphys. In October 1943 the corporate
life of the old Murphy Transfer Company, founded in 1913, came to an
end and the Murphys, Spellacy, and American Bank's voting trust
were joined in a new struggle for control of the parent company.

3

'Around-the-Corner Folska'

N THE EARLY 1940s, Ed Murphy, the third E. L. Murphy, re-membered, "I had one foot in the law firm and the other in the E. L. Murphy Trucking Company, helping to keep the company going as my father recovered from two heart attacks. The first was in December 1941, and there was another the following spring. My mother May was there, too, but soon I was at the trucking company almost full-time. It was apparent that my father wasn't going to be

The third Edward L. (Ed) Murphy in 1945, the year he and his father regained control of Murphy Transfer and Storage and Murphy Motor Freight Lines and Ed Murphy became president of the companies.

able to work for awhile. I was the oldest son, my brother Dick was eighteen and in the army. Fur-thermore, I liked the business. I'd driven trucks for Murphy Motor Freight when I was a college stu-dent—my favorite route was the Twin Cities-to-Duluth run—so it was obvious that I needed to leave the practice of law and join the trucking company."

In 1943, an outdated provision in state law set in motion a series of life-changing events for the Murphy family. When the Murphy Transfer Com-pany was incorporated in 1913, state law estab-lished a corporation's lifetime as thirty years. The law also stipulated that at the end of that thirty-year period, all stockholders had to vote either to renew the incorporation or to liquidate the

69

company. Although the Murphy Transfer name had been changed to Murphy Transfer and Storage Company in 1919, and the law was amended later to allow a corporation to function in perpetuity, Murphy Transfer Company was grandfathered in under the old statute.

E. L. Murphy Sr., had held onto his stock in Murphy Transfer throughout the turmoil surrounding the loss of the company in 1935. Eight years later, when all stockholders had to agree to renew the corporation, the Murphys, father and son, conferred. Ed Murphy remembered it well:

A page from the handwritten notes of Edward L. Murphy Sr., tracing the history of Murphy Motor Freight Lines and its parent company, Murphy Transfer and Storage. Murphy jotted down these notes on September 9, 1953.

My father received notice that one of the issues involved in the bank's voting trust was extending the life of Murphy Transfer Company. After talking with Perry Moore, the partner who had brought me into the law firm, I told my father that even though Ibar Spellacy and the bank could control Murphy Transfer and Murphy Motor Freight Lines through the voting trust, they didn't have the power to extend the life of the corporation. Only the stockholders could do that.

The stage was set for a series of manuevers aimed at restoring control of Murphy Transfer and Murphy Motor Freight Lines to the Murphys. Ed Murphy, who at the time was listed by the ICC as vice president of E. L. Murphy Trucking Company, also held a small amount of E. L. Murphy stock. Now he turned over his shares to his father, giving him full control of E. L. Murphy Trucking as they planned for a buyout they both felt was increasingly possible.

First they would need a co-investor, and Ed Murphy turned to his father's old friend, Stanley L. Wasie, president of Merchants Motor Freight. Wasie's background in trucking was impressive. He was a founder of Transport Clearings of the Twin Cities, a past president of the American Trucking Association, and a founder and chairman of the Middlewest Motor Freight Bureau.

"In 1936, when dad was starting E. L. Murphy Trucking Company," Ed Murphy recalled, "Stan Wasie loaned him $1,500, which was a lot of money in the depths of the depression. So I called on Wasie and explained the corporate life situation and the opportunity it presented. Stan was interested. We worked out an agreement that he would put in half of the money—$35,000— and I would add the other half (which I had to borrow, with Joe Shiely, my father-in-law, as guarantor) and we'd try to buy back Murphy Transfer and Motor Freight Lines."

Edward L. Murphy Sr., fired the opening gun in the litigation that followed. Exercising his right as a stockholder, he refused to vote to renew the corporate life of Murphy Transfer. Then he transferred his stock in the company to his son to strengthen his hand in the coming negotiations. In November 1944, Ed Murphy filed a lawsuit charging the bank, the voting trust, and Spellacy with mismanagement of Murphy Transfer and Murphy Motor Freight Lines, and with "failure to take advantage of opportunities."

While this was a move to get everyone's attention, there was some substance to the charge, Ed Murphy remembered. As the depression lifted and World War II broke out, the trucking industry was doing well in its vital role of meeting a pent-up demand for goods and services and hauling troops, equipment, and supplies for the armed forces. Ed Murphy felt, however, that Murphy Transfer and Murphy Motor Freight "were kind of dogging along, not doing much, while their competitors were making money. The company books were showing $482,252 in assets and liabilities and Wasie and I were convinced the companies could be run better and do well. The success story of Murphy Motor Freight Lines in the following years is the best evidence that the company was not, in fact, being managed as well as it might have been."

The office of Murphy Motor Freight Lines at 480 Broadway in St. Paul's Lowertown around 1948.

There was another factor in the Murphys' favor. Although American Bank's voting trust actually had been controlling the operations of Murphy Transfer and Motor Freight Lines since 1935, the company had not been able to pay off the money the bank loaned it back in the 1920s to build the two warehouses. The result was that American was balking at advancing any more money.

"American was anxious to get out," Ed Murphy remembered. "That's called a 'work out' situation—trying to find a way out of a problem."

At 2 P.M. on November 27, 1944 a special meeting of the board of directors of Murphy Motor Freight Lines, Inc., was held in St. Paul. With Ibar Spellacy as president, and Joseph A. Lethert, acting as secretary, the board agreed to a settlement with the plaintiffs. In stilted legalese, the minutes of that meeting recorded the decision.

> WHEREAS, E. L. Murphy, also known as E. L. Murphy Jr., did prior hereto commence an action against the Murphy Motor Freight Lines, Incorporated, and others which action is now pending, and

> WHEREAS, it seems to be for the best interest of said corporation that said litigation be settled and compromised, and

> WHEREAS, E. L. Murphy and the officers of this corporation and the other defendants in said action have negotiated a contract of settlement which is hereinafter set forth, and

A line-up of Murphy Motor Freight trucks at 480 Broadway.

WHEREAS, it appears for the best interest of this corporation that said contract be in all things approved and the President and Secretary of this corporation be authorized to execute the same on behalf of the corporation. . . .

A many-page Agreement of Settlement followed. It was clear, Ed Murphy recalled, that the bank had not wanted to deal with a lawsuit.

> On the other hand, we didn't have the money to fight them. We did have the money to buy out Spellacy, his 150 shares of stock in Murphy Transfer and his 766 shares in Murphy Motor Freight, and we did so. We also picked up fifty-three shares of Murphy Motor Freight Lines stock held by Harry Humason as trustee of the voting trust. Spellacy didn't want to lose the company. He felt very strongly about that. I think, however, that American realized there was a solid buyer out there who could pay off the bank, and simply told Spellacy that this was the end of the line.

On May 21, 1945, the Murphys regained control of Murphy Transfer & Storage Company, the parent company of Murphy Motor Freight Lines. As Ed Murphy remembered it,

> That was the day I walked back into the company and said "there has been a transfer of control of the business from Mr. Spellacy and the American National Bank to Stan Wasie and myself, with my having been elected president today. We

purchased the interest held by both Spellacy and American National Bank. We believe this company has a great future and we will make every effort to improve all phases of the operation and will provide the necessary funds to do that. The company can operate profitably, but it must have your full cooperation and best efforts. Every person here will benefit from a new start. I am very optimistic that we can achieve that objective." Then we moved immediately to renew the corporate life of the Murphy Transfer Company.

Officers were elected: E. L. Murphy Sr., president, and lawyer M. J. Doherty, secretary and treasurer. First National Bank of St. Paul already had supplanted American as banker for E. L.Murphy Trucking Company. Embarking on its renewed corporate life, Murphy Transfer Company issued promissory notes to its purchasers, Stan Wasie, and Edward Murphy.

For E. L. Murphy Sr., whose stock had been the lever the Murphys used to pry loose the company from Spellacy and the bank, it was a bitter victory. His presidency of Murphy Transfer and Murphy Motor

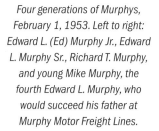

Four generations of Murphys, February 1, 1953. Left to right: Edward L. (Ed) Murphy Jr., Edward L. Murphy Sr., Richard T. Murphy, and young Mike Murphy, the fourth Edward L. Murphy, who would succeed his father at Murphy Motor Freight Lines.

A large circular diesel engine after it was installed. Murphy Rigging and Erecting Company hauled the engine to a plant in Milaca, Minnesota.

Freight Lines was short-lived. On May 21, 1945, Ed Murphy resigned as secretary of E. L. Murphy Trucking Company to become president of Murphy Transfer and Murphy Motor Freight. Stanley Wasie was named vice president. It was another heart-breaking episode in the senior Murphy's life.

"My father felt that because he had contributed the stock, there always would be a job for him at Murphy Motor Freight," Dick Murphy explained. "It was not to be." Ed Murphy remembered with anguish his father's anger and disappointment:

> It was never intended that Dad remain president of the Transfer and Motor Freight company. Wasie wanted only one partner to deal with and he said he wouldn't invest the money unless it was set up that way. We didn't have any other way to get the money we needed. Dad had every right to be angry about it, but he still had E. L. Murphy Trucking Company to run and he'd just recovered from two heart attacks.

There was a practical side to the emotional trauma. Two different types of trucking companies were involved. Murphy Motor Freight Lines had been certified by the ICC as operating a regular route system between the Twin Cities, Duluth, and other terminals. It was a regular-route (LTL) carrier, using the same routes every day. "If a customer had 500 pounds of freight to haul, we picked it up and delivered it," Ed Murphy explained. "We did a little business with many

RAILROADS AND THE TRUCKING INDUSTRY

When railroad construction in the United States took off after the Civil War, the railroads gradually overtook ship and barge traffic on the nation's inland waterways and the Great Lakes as the major carrier of domestic freight traffic. The expansion of the nation's railroad network peaked in 1916 when the railroads hauled 77 percent of the nation's intercity freight traffic. That year the United States Congress established the country's first federal highway program with legislation that provided a federal match to state dollars spent for new federal highways. By the 1920s, the trucking industry began to challenge both railroads and inland waterways as an intercity freight carrier.

The gradual passage of state and federal laws in the 1920s levying gas taxes to finance the construction of new and improved highways helped spur the growth of the trucking industry. The greater flexibility and convenience trucks offered first took the hauling of less-than-carload lots away from the railroads.

By 1940, according to Transportation in America *by Rosalyn Wilson, the railroads were carrying 370 billions of ton miles, or 61.3 percent of the United States' domestic freight, while trucks hauled sixty-two billions of ton miles, or 10 percent of the freight. During the five years spanned by World War II, railroad tonnage almost doubled, to 697.3 billions of ton miles, or 67 percent of the nation's freight, while the trucking industry's share fell to 6.5 percent. However, five years later in 1950 the statistics began to reflect the decline of the rails and the upward movement of trucks as carriers: 597 billions of ton miles for the rails, or 56.2 percent; 173 billions of ton miles for trucks, or 16.3 percent. The pattern of trucks overtaking railroads in carrying domestic freight would continue throughout the 1950s and 1960s. By 1970 railroads would be carrying 771 billions of ton miles, or 39.8 percent, and trucks 412 billions of ton miles, or 21.3 percent. The Murphy Companies rode this wave for more than fifty years.*

customers." E. L. Murphy Trucking Company, on the other hand, was in the local cartage and heavy hauling business, a more-than-a-truckload operation known as an irregular route common carrier.

"My father was really comfortable with the local cartage business," Ed Murphy remembered. "I don't think that running Murphy Motor Freight and E. L. Murphy Trucking Company together would have been a good mix for him. His heart was in local cartage and heavy hauling, not the common carrier business."

In December 1946, a reorganization took place. As recorded in the minutes of a special meeting of Murphy Motor Freight's board, the directors approved a proposed exchange of Murphy Motor Freight's assets and liabilities with Murphy Transfer & Storage Company, in return for the capital stock held by Murphy Transfer. Ed Murphy, who was authorized to finalize the transaction, explained it:

> I wanted to simplify a hierarchy that wasn't serving any purpose after 1945 because Dad had the local business and the

heavy hauling, and the over-the-road business remained with Murphy Motor Freight Lines. My thought was to merge Murphy Transfer and Murphy Motor Freight, but keep Murphy Transfer as the surviving company. So I put Murphy Motor Freight into the Murphy Transfer Company. Although I changed the Transfer name to Murphy Motor Freight Lines, I really extinguished Murphy Motor Freight. The company actually was Murphy Transfer with a new name. I know it sounds confusing, but it worked.

A Garage across from the Depot

Since its founding in 1936, E. L. Murphy Trucking Company had been functioning independently as a co-partnership. On January 28, 1946, the company filed new incorporation papers, with E. L. Murphy Sr., listed as president and treasurer. May Murphy as vice president filled the vacancy created by Ed Murphy's resignation; Richard T. Murphy, now twenty-two and a student at the University of Minnesota, was secretary.

Other organizational matters were dealt with that year, according to the minutes. In January, the E. L. Murphy Trucking Company co-partnership turned over to the newly incorporated E. L. Murphy Trucking Company all of its business assets and property in exchange for 4,400 shares of the corporation's capital stock; 1,000 shares went to E. L. Murphy Sr., 500 shares to E. L. Murphy Jr., and 2,900 shares to Richard T. Murphy. The next month, Ed Murphy turned over his shares to May Murphy. The corporation's board of directors again named the senior Murphy president and treasurer, May Murphy vice president, and Richard T. Murphy, secretary. The following April 23, the company was incorporated in Iowa.

At Murphy Motor Freight, on September 16, 1948, Ed Murphy opened a new $250,000 terminal building at 965 Eustis Street with more than 3,700 guests attending an open house. "The evening festivities," the press noted, "were highlighted by an appearance of Cedric Adams, the popular local columnist and radio newsman, who acted as master of ceremonies and conducted his evening broadcast from the terminal."

Trade publications described the terminal as a 50,000 square-foot structure on a three-and-a-half-acre lot with loading facilities for thirty to thirty-five units and an outside dock for an additional twenty trailers. The terminal included a 450-foot conveyor unit or "carousel"

E. L. Murphy Trucking Company at 1924 University Avenue, before its move to to Roseville in the early 1950s. Photo from Murphy Warehouse Company.

Richard T. Murphy, Sr.

I have had a long and wonderful experience working and living in the Midway district. As a child, I grew up on its fringe, a block away from the College of St. Thomas, and my father, in 1936, moved his business, E. L. Murphy Trucking Company, from Minneapolis to a location at 1924 University Avenue.

This was just close enough for me to ride my bike to the office after school or, during the winter months, walk from St. Mark's school to the office so that I could begin to learn what it was to work. This was around 1937. After school, it was my job to fuel all the trucks and back them into the garage for parking. After that, I checked oil, aired tires and did anything else the shop foreman asked of me. For this I received the princely sum of 50 cents per week. Wow! I had more spending money than most of my friends. This set me on the road to a career that has been fulfilling, richly rewarding and much loved.

My first recollections of the Prior and University area were of the team track operated by the Minnesota Transfer Railway on the southwest corner and of our own building located in the middle of the block to the east. Across the street, the Midway Club had its offices on the sec-

ond floor of the Esslinger building. This was a multiple story, older type of building with a cafe and bar on the first floor. I'm not sure who the other tenants in the upper floors were.

Next to this was a machine shop called Lloyd Products. Its owner was a former Navy veteran who apparently was highly skilled at tool and die-making. I recall seeing him in the area frequently. Always driving a large Lincoln or Pierce Arrow automobile replete with white wall tires mounted on the sides just ahead of the front doors. He always seemed to have a cigar in his mouth. Next to us was the H. V. Smith Company. Smith was in the extermination business, and I never really understood what that was all about.

Our company, in those days, was in the machinery moving and local cartage business. Dad had an extensive fleet of motor vehicles that operated up and down University Avenue between the warehouse and rail areas adjacent to the "loops" in both Minneapolis and St. Paul. In addition, we delivered orders to the homes of Sears Roebuck's customers—a myriad of wonderful things, none of which we seemingly could afford.

Saturdays were big days at our company because every truck had to be washed and swept out. Guess who headed up that project. I would start at 6

a.m. and usually work until 6 or 7 in the evening in order to complete the job. The highlight of the day was my father taking me across the street to Esslinger's cafe for lunch. Boy, did I eat well!

I graduated from St. Mark's in 1937, and went on to high school at St. Thomas Military Academy. This was then located on the college campus so I could continue my afternoon routine. During the summer, I was able to work fulltime and earned the handsome amount of $2 per week; half of that had to be placed in a savings account at what was then First Security State Bank located at Raymond and University.

I graduated from St. Thomas in June of 1942 and, much to my surprise, was commissioned a second lieutenant in the United States Army as a result of my military training at St. Thomas. During my senior year, Congress had lowered the age for commissioned officers from twenty-one to eighteen, and on June 4 I not only received my high school diploma but also my commission. A scant ten days later I was at Camp Wolters, Texas, assigned to an infantry replacement training unit.

After service in the Army and subsequently the Army Air Corps, I returned from the war in 1945 and enrolled at the University of Minnesota.

The E. L. Murphy Trucking Company office at 1924 University in the late 1940s. With it is a portion of a reminiscence by Dick Murphy published in Ramsey County History.

to handle freight. It was, Murphy said, "the first of its kind in the Twin Cities area and the third of its kind in the United States."

In 1948 Dick Murphy joined E. L. Murphy Trucking as a dispatcher. He was scarcely new to the business. His first recollection of the company was its location "in a garage that was part of a building the company rented in Minneapolis on the north side of the river and across from the old railroad depot. We were there for a short time before moving to 1924 University."

His memories of those early years and of working as a youngster for his father provide a glimpse into the company as it was during the late 1930s. Company headquarters at 1924 University Avenue in St. Paul's Midway district were close enough to the Murphy home on Exeter Place for him to walk or ride his bike to the office "and begin to learn what it was to work. I was only about thirteen years old, but after school and on Saturdays it was my job to fuel all the trucks and back them into the garage for parking. After that I checked oil, aired tires, and did anything else the shop foreman asked of me. For this I received the princely sum of 50 cents per week, but I had more spending money than most of my friends and those early experiences set me on the road to a career that has been fulfilling, richly rewarding, and much loved."

A story from those years has embedded itself in family memories. It concerns a dispatcher the family called "Around-the-Corner" Folska, a great friend of the senior Murphy from the Rice Street neighborhood. Dick Murphy remembered him:

> He always wore a fedora and he carried a flask in his breast pocket. He chewed tobacco constantly and he had his spittoon right by his desk. He was a great dispatcher, but he never wrote anything down. Had it all in his head. If a customer called to ask "Where's the truck? The truck isn't here," his stock answer was "Look out the window. It's coming around the corner." That's how he got his name.

Dick Murphy remembered his father's "extensive fleet of trucks" moving up and down University Avenue between the warehouse districts of Minneapolis and St. Paul. In addition, "We delivered orders to the homes of Sears, Roebuck's customers—a myriad of wonderful things, none of which we seemingly could afford."

> Saturdays were big days. Every truck had to be washed and swept out. Even as a teenager I managed that project. I would start at 6 a.m. and usually work until 6 or 7 in the evening to complete the job. The highlight of the day was my father taking me across the street to Esslinger's café and sometimes to Napoleon's for lunch. I ate well.

He remembered that when he was a student at the University of Minnesota and working part-time at the company, "I had a rather ingenious method of transportation."

In the early morning, I would catch a ride in one of the Murphy trucks that was heading into Minneapolis. In the afternoon, when I finished classes, I would simply go to University and Fifteenth Avenue Southeast, wait on the corner and flag down the first Murphy truck that came along. The driver would stop, pick me up, and take me to the office where I changed my clothes and resumed my gofer duties.

I vividly remember being sent to Midway Transfer's team track with instructions to supervise the unloading of the famous Tucker motor car. This was a radically designed new approach to motor vehicles, and it was being sent around the country on a promotion tour. When I opened the boxcar, I stood in awe of this magnificent vehicle with its "cyclops" headlight and other aerodynamic features—obviously way ahead of its time. However, I discovered the car couldn't be operated because it didn't have an engine. With a lot of pushing and shoving, we got it out of the boxcar, into a truck, and down to the St. Paul Auditorium for exhibition.

Moving a linotype for the St. Paul Pioneer Press and Dispatch on December 18, 1940. The newspaper hired Murphy Rigging to move this heavy linotype typesetting machine from an upper floor in its old building to the paper's new facility. By knocking out a section of the exterior wall, the Murphy crew was able to lower the linotype onto a waiting truck without having to disassemble the machine, thereby making the move quickly.

THE SAINT PAUL PIONEER PRESS. SUNDAY, DECEMBE

Watch Out Below—Heavy Linotype Lowered

Having prospered during World War II, along with the trucking industry in general, E. L. Murphy Trucking began to expand into hauling more of the heavy, cumbersome articles for such companies as 3M, Honeywell, and American Hoist & Derrick. War's end brought new demands, new opportunities, this time for goods that had been unavailable during the bleak years of depression and war. The company was making money. It was serving ten other states, besides Minnesota: the Dakotas, Montana, Iowa, Missouri, Wisconsin, Illinois, Indiana, Ohio, and Michigan, and it was poised for the major expansion that would come in the 1960s.

After four years as a dispatcher, Dick Murphy was named executive vice president in 1951 and placed in line "to serve as president in the event the president was unable to serve." A year later Edward L. Murphy Sr., became chairman of the board of directors. Dick Murphy, at the age of twenty-seven, became president of E. L. Murphy Trucking Company and eligible for membership in the Young Presidents Organization, a new, prestigious, nationwide group for young business executives that had been founded in New York in 1950. The Twin Cities Chapter was established the following year with twenty-three members, among them Ed Murphy, who had become president of Murphy Motor Freight when he was twenty-nine. Criteria for membership included "presidency of an industrial corporation with $8 million in annual sales and at least 100 employees, or head of a service firm doing a $2 million business yearly with a minimum of fifty employees." All before the age of thirty-nine. Dick Murphy would become treasurer of the Twin Cities YPO chapter in 1959.

On May 29, 1948, Murphy had married Helen Duffy, the third of three young St. Paul women who were known as "the beautiful Duffy girls"—Mary, who married Joseph Hines and later Reinny Bohlman,

Mired in mud. E. L. Murphy trucks sink deep into the mud while trying to move an American Thunderbolt and a German light bomber from Wold-Chamberlain Air Field in Minneapolis to the Minneapolis Auditorium. The planes were part of a display for the opening of the Northwest Aviation Show. A third truck with heavy tow lines worked for hours to free the planes.

THE WINTER CARNIVAL

"Perhaps the people down in the states imagine that we of Minnesota go into a state of torpidity during our long and severe winters, like the frogs and snakes of their own swamps and marshes," the Minnesota Chronicle and Register *speculated on December 22, 1849, when Minnesota was not yet a state. But, the writer assured his readers, nothing could be further from the truth.*

It would be another thirty-seven years, however, before St. Paul's first Winter Carnival in 1886 proved his point, even though through the years, the Carnival has operated in fits and starts that occasionally included unseasonably warm winters that melted ice castles. In 1916 Louis W. Hill breathed new life into the Carnival when he declared, according to the St. Paul Pioneer Press, *that "Men who cannot forget their business and get out and take part in the Winter Carnival are not the kind of men we want in St. Paul."*

The depression of the 1930s dimmed enthusiasm for carnivals in general, but in St. Paul by 1937 a great ice castle, a symmetric modern pavilion designed by Clarence W. Wigington, was going up in Central Park. The outbreak of World War II brought a somber military note to the 1942 carnival. A year after the "Victory Carnival" of 1946, when Helen Duffy (Murphy) became Winter Carnival queen, the carnival was back to stay, even though the ice palace melted with less than a third of it completed. From then on, St. Paul's Winter Carnival would loom as a major annual event in the lives of Dick and Helen Murphy and their family.

Richard T. Murphy, Sr. as captain of King Boreas' Royal Guard for 1949. Pioneer Press *photo.*

and Eileen, who married Richard Donovan of the Donovan Construction Company. Born and raised in St. Paul and Irish to the core, Helen Duffy was queen of St. Paul's Winter Carnival in 1947. When she asked Dick Murphy to be her escort, a romance blossomed that seems to have captivated St. Paul. "People still remember that," Carole Faricy said.

Not long after their wedding at St. Mark's Church, Dick Murphy was sent off to northern Minnesota to manage a major project for the company. Changes were sweeping through the mining industry as ore deposits, including those on Minnesota's Mesabi iron range, began to play out. Bethlehem Steel was building a taconite plant at Hoyt Lakes in a massive effort to extract an iron oxide ore from taconite, the hard mother-rock of the Mesabi iron range. Taconite Harbor—its huge docks stretching out into the Lake Superior—was under contruction north of Two Harbors. As Dick Murphy remembered it, the trucking company's contract came through a friend of his who was a traffic manager for Bethlehem Steel in Chicago.

It was a rigorous assignment that stretched across the better part of four years. "We were subcontractors for the steel company," Murphy said. "We didn't haul any taconite. Our job was to haul the steel and machinery needed to build the facility at Hoyt Lakes, construct the docks at Taconite Harbor, and build a railroad linking Hoyt Lakes and nearby Aurora with Lake Superior. The rails came into Aurora. There wasn't any railroad to Taconite Harbor until the steel company built it. We hauled in the rails and the ties, the roofing, and the machinery—you name it. I supervised the trucking company crews, and it was an immense job."

Murphy found himself spending five, sometimes six, days a week between Taconite Harbor and Hoyt Lakes. "I'd leave the house early Monday morning and drive to Duluth. I had to be gone all week. We often worked Saturdays. Dad just insisted that 'when they work, you're there, damn it, that's your job.'"

He had a trailer in Hoyt Lakes and another in Taconite Harbor. "Bethlehem Steel put in hundreds of trailers for people working at those sites. Wherever I was at the end of my workday, that's where I'd stay. There weren't any hotels or motels, although I did have a room at the Agate Bay hotel in Two Harbors and I also had my office there. That's when I fell in love with the North Shore and thought someday I'd like to live there. We went to a ma-and-pa resort, Barthell's, for years, before I bought land and built a cabin on Lake Superior."

TACONITE AND THE MESABI RANGE

Iron ore was discovered in northeastern Minnesota in the late 1860s, but the shipping of this vital industrial resource did not begin until 1884. It would be another six years before the Merritt brothers—the "Seven Iron Men"—began the mining in 1890 of the rich Mesabi (an Ojibwe word meaning hidden giant*) Range in St. Louis County. With its two other iron ranges, the smaller Vermilion and Cuyuna, Minnesota would become the richest source of iron ore in the world. Ore from the vast Mesabi Range alone soon produced more than 70 percent of all the ore from all the iron mines clustered around Lake Superior.*

It was not to last. Iron ore was not a renewable resource. Within sixty years the Mesabi's high grade ore, known as hematite and almost 60 percent pure iron, was facing depletion, spurred by surging demand during the World War II years. The industry turned to taconite. A team of researchers at the University of Minnesota's Mines Experiment Station had found a way to extract the 25 to 35 percent iron ore content of taconite, the mother rock which formed the Mesabi's iron ore deposits, and turn it into pellets that could be shipped on to steel manufacturers. By the mid-1950s taconite plants had sprung up along the Mesabi, bringing a renaissance to the existing range towns and creating others, such as Hoyt Lakes, where E. L. Murphy Trucking Company hauled supplies for a new railroad.

'... *Your Eyeballs Bounced*'

The Hoyt Lakes project finally completed in 1952, Murphy went back to work in the St. Paul office where he began to make far-ranging plans for building the business. Among those plans was the incorporation in 1956 of the Murphy Warehouse Company he had founded in 1952. He saw a different future for the company than did his father. Events at the national level were coalescing to usher in a golden era for the trucking industry. Winding, crooked roads where trucks couldn't pass were being replaced by four-lane highways. The 1956 Federal Aid Highway Act authored the creation of a 41,000-mile interstate system, ideal for trucks and paving the way for the trucking industry to overtake the railroads in transporting goods.

Trucks were undergoing massive overhauls, too. Long gone were the lumbering vehicles of the Murphys' early days in the 1920s and 1930s, when "trucks were so utilitarian that it was difficult keeping your eyes on the road," as one veteran driver graphically described them. "You bounced like on springs; the roads were just awful. You bounced so bad your eyeballs bounced. You couldn't see where you were going. It was something I'd like to forget."

Lighter trucks, but with more power and offering smoother rides and more comfort for drivers, were rolling off the assembly lines. By the 1950s trucks with 275-HP supercharged engines had been developed for use on the West Coast. With sleeper cabs added, one person could sleep as another drove, keeping loads moving constantly and boosting profits. As the years wore on, wider trailers made from aluminum and fiberglass would become the norm and trucks fitted with television sets, cell phones, microwaves, and other electronic gear would truly become "homes-on-wheels." All that lay in the future, however.

In the meantime, at Murphy Motor Freight Lines, Ed Murphy was devoting 99 percent of his time to the company. In addition, he was elected a director of the St. Paul Chamber of Commerce, of First Security Bank and of First National Bank, both of St. Paul, and president of Midwest Motor Transport Association (MMTA). Following in his father's footsteps, he was appointed one of six new directors of the Twin Cities Rapid Transit Company. It was a move by a group of Twin Cities civic and business leaders to replace TCRT's earlier management that had been been accused of dishonesty and inefficiency. A major issue the new board faced was a fare increase to keep the cities' transportation system running. Commenting in the Twin Cities newspapers on his appointment, Murphy observed that

Taconite mining at the Erie Mining Company, Hoyt Lakes, Minnesota, around 1955. For the better part of four years, Dick Murphy managed an E. L. Murphy Trucking Company project there. As sub-contractor for Bethlehem Steel that was building a taconite plant at Hoyt Lakes, the Murphy company hauled the steel and machinery for constructing a railroad linking Hoyt Lakes and Lake Superior. Minnesota Historical Society photograph.

"I look at it as a civic project. I'm willing to offer my help. We are all trying to help the Transit Company be as good as it can be. We will have to study the thing from top to bottom and determine what can be done."

At the same time, Dick Murphy was taking the first steps in steering E. L. Murphy Trucking Company away from the local cartage business. "I could see," he explained, "that the local hauling business was nickel-and-dime stuff."

> You couldn't make any money because the rates you charged were so low and the profit margin minimal. On the other hand, E. L. Murphy Trucking already was hauling machinery, picking it up at warehouses and taking it to other warehouses, and we had that authority from the ICC to haul safes and vault doors around Minnesota, the Dakotas, and the rest of the Upper Midwest. It just occurred to me, why don't we expand on that? I thought we could make more money if we were hauling interstate. Dad was relectant to get into that because we were at least paying the bills and even though it had been thirty years ago, he was still shaken by the loss of Murphy Transfer and Murphy Motor Freight back in 1935. But eventually I prevailed over his fears and objections.

TRUCKS AND TERMINALS

St. Paul's Midway District, where E. L. Murphy Trucking Company and Murphy Motor Freight Lines established their offices and terminals in the 1930s, was at that time the fourth largest trucking center in the country. Trucks hauling goods nosed out of the Twin Cities to reach into far-flung communities not served by the railroads.

During the post-World War II era, these over-the-road trucks followed miles of newly built highways and freeways that linked the metro-

politan region with the rest of the country. And the nearby northern St. Paul suburb of Roseville, where the Murphy companies came to rest in the 1960s, became one of the most important truck terminals in the Twin Cities region.

By the mid-1980s the Minnesota Motor Transport Association would list about half of the trucks registered in the state as panels, light pick-ups, and delivery vans. The rest were truck tractors and heavier straight trucks.

I acquired another set of authorities, in addition to the one for Diebold and then I just kept applying for authority as I found customers who had products to haul. I was filing applications right and left with the ICC and then I'd go to all those hearings. When I finished those filings, I had 118 ICC certificates. That's how I built the business. Once we got out of the local hauling business, we really began to make money.

The E. L. Murphy Trucking Company was becoming one of the premier specialized heavy-hauling companies in the nation. In 1956 Dick Murphy helped organize the Heavy Specialized Carriers Conference; he became its first president and received an award for "a job well done" in winning recognition of the conference by the Local Cartage National Conference Board. On June 27, 1957, in a hearing held in Minneapolis, the ICC granted Murphy Trucking the authority to operate in thirty-four more states. In her minutes, company secretary May Murphy noted that: "This gives us the entire country to operate in, except the states of Washington, Oregon, and Idaho" and "Mr. Murphy reported that these three states could still be served by means of the Heavy and Specialized Carriers 'Red Book' operation."

Two years later, in 1959, as the largest heavy-specialized carrier in the Upper Midwest, E. L. Murphy Trucking entered the Space Age when it hauled a seven-ton special space cabin simulator from Minnesota to Texas. The space capsule, eight feet high and twelve feet long, was built by the Aeronautical Division of Minneapolis Honeywell for the Department of Astroecology of the Air Force School of Aviation at Brooks Air Force Base in San Antonio. The first of its kind, and known as "the world's smallest efficiency apartment," the capsule

Changing color schemes. The Murphy companies were noted for the changing colors of their trucks, although green often was dominant. These have green tops and lettering.

was designed to simulate living conditions for two men for a month in space, according to an article in the November 1959, issue of *American Cartagemen*. The capsule had "all the comforts of home," at least whatever comforts were deemed necessary in those pioneer planning years for space travel: "executive-chairs, bed, sanitary facilities, food, cooking equipment," and a maze of scientific instruments.

The magazine described how Murphy transported not only the capsule, but also its control panel and delicate instruments. The company equipped a twenty-five-foot single-axle trailer with special springs and additional shock absorbers and selected an International 190 tractor, also equipped with air-conditioned shock absorbers, to pull the trailer. Arriving in San Antonio, "Murphy's experts unloaded it, moved it through two widened doorways for about 200 feet, raised it up and over a four-foot counter and erected it in upright position." The magazine added that "The [Murphy] Company owns and operates 276 pieces of equipment and can handle at a moment's notice anything up to 150 tons."

Several years later, E. L. Murphy Trucking hauled ninety-four-foot prestressed girders, the heaviest and the largest bridge beams for the longest bridge to be built in Minnesota up to the 1960s. The forty-ton, four-and-a-half-foot girders were hauled two a day on semi-trailer trucks the ninety miles from Roseville, where they were manufactured by Prestressed Concrete, Inc., to New Ulm where a new bridge would carry Highway 14 across the Minnesota River.

A long article in the October 1969, issue of the monthly trade magazine, *Transportation Engineer*, described E. L. Murphy Trucking Company as it was during the 1960s, that period of massive economic growth for the nation and of booming expansion for the company. Companies such as FMC, Honeywell, and Minneapolis Moline that had provided guns and large vehicles to the armed forces during World War II had continued to supply defense needs during the Cold War period. As these manufacturers prospered by filling orders from the Department of Defense, so did E. L. Murphy Trucking Company by delivering their heavy equipment. The consumer economy grew too, with companies such as Toro and its snowblowers depending on Murphy Trucking to warehouse their products and deliver them to customers. Dick Murphy designed a special trailer to haul the snowmobiles that Toro manufactured.

As the 1960s drew to a close, the trucking company had become

Hauling bindery equipment, a 20-ton machine for Brown and Bigelow in June, 1945.

one of the fastest growing entities in the Murphy organization—so much so that in 1967 Dick Murphy decided to abandon entirely local cartage and heavy hauling to concentrate on heavy specialized hauling around the country. The future, he explained, belonged to heavy hauling because "it's the second fastest-growing form of trucking. Only the hauling of refrigerated loads is growing at a faster pace."

He already had broad authority to operate as a heavy specialized carrier for commodities that required special equipment or special handling, or both, in the forty-eight continental states. In fact, he told *Transportation Engineer,* 70 percent of the trucking company's volume came from non-permit loads—loads that called for special equipment to load and unload but could be carried legally without special permits.

Dick Murphy, by this time, was heading four companies. E. L. Murphy Trucking was the largest of his operations, and it had two subsidiaries. First there was Murphy Rigging and Erecting, a crane and rigging company that was almost a heavy construction company in itself. It was in the throes of its own expansion, adding two 110-ton trailers, widening the area it serviced by accepting assignments outside the Upper Midwest, and increasing its scope by offering a turnkey service. Not only did Murphy Rigging and Erecting deliver the equipment but the company also set it up, complete with wiring. All the owner needed to do was to turn it on.

Murphy Rigging also provided an ongoing maintenance and repair service, Dick Murphy said. "Customers were demanding maintenance because the machines and their maintenance had grown far more complex. The companies we were serving didn't have field repair people of their own."

Second, there was Murphy Delivery Service that did contract hauling for Sears, Roebuck. It had been part of the trucking company since 1937 when, under Edward Murphy Sr., "We began hauling refrigerators for Sears. We delivered anything Sears sold and its customers wanted delivered, especially such large packages as washers, dryers, refrigerators, and furniture," Dick Murphy remembered. Finally, there was Murphy Warehouse Company, a freestanding, separate corporation of its own and an operation that unloaded merchandise from trucks and trains, stored it, handled it with forklifts, and shipped it in warehouse trucks to customers upon demand.

In 1967 Murphy decided to reorganize, splitting off Murphy Rigging and Erecting and Murphy Delivery Service from the parent company and setting them up as separate corporations under the Murphy banner. He explained his decision:

Maroon and cream. Beginning in the 1930s, the Murphys' diesel tractors carried this combination of maroon and cream. This photo from the 1940s shows a tractor trailer hauling a piece of heavy equipment. E. L. Murphy Sr., is on the right.

E. L. Murphy Trucking was standing on its own as a premier heavy specialized hauling company. It didn't make sense to keep Murphy Rigging and Erecting as part of the trucking company because people who knew trucking didn't know anything about rigging. And it also didn't make sense to have Murphy Delivery operating within a trucking company

On February 13, 1967, he announced the change. Citing the growth in the economy since the early 1960s and the extensive ICC authority the trucking company had acquired, he pointed to the need to expand the company's other operations. The two new corporations, he said, would be owned completely by the E. L. Murphy Trucking Company. All functions relating to machinery moving, rigging and erecting would now be managed by the new Rigging and Erecting corporation. Murphy Delivery Service would handle "all functions relating to deliveries for Sears." Then he explained the labor issues that were involved:

> The collective bargaining agreement with General Drivers Union Local 120 that covered the company's Line Haul, Local Cartage, Local Heavy Handling would be transferred to Murphy Rigging and Erecting. The contract with General Drivers Union 544 for the Sears deliveries would be transferred to Murphy Delivery Service. A rider negotiated four years earlier with Local 120, permitting E. L. Murphy Trucking Company to lease independent drivers for road activities, would remain with the trucking company.

John Solum, who joined E. L. Murphy Trucking in 1946 as a dispatcher and rose to the position of vice president and general manager, remembered the 1950s and 1960s when for E. L. Murphy Sr., "the Sears account was his pride and joy." And no wonder. In its heyday, Sears was the largest retailer in the United States, the economic engine that provided jobs and services for thousands of small companies all across the country. Murphy Delivery maintained a small, one-room office, staffed with a supervisor, at the Sears building on Lake Street in Minneapolis. "E. L. Murphy used to take me with him when he called on Sears," Solum recalled.

Murphy Motor Freight delivery
points listed on the backs of
1940s Motor Freight trucks.

He drove a Chevrolet on those calls. Although he liked Cadillacs, he used a smaller car when he went to Sears because he didn't want the customers to know that he owned a Cadillac. He was probably the best-dressed man in the Twin Cities, too. He always wore a suit, tie, and a shirt with French cuffs. Apparently his wife, May, once told him not to wear colored shirts because all successful men wore white shirts.

The Delivery Service, however, came under scrutiny at a special meeting of the trucking company's board of directors on September 3, 1973. Chaired by Dick Murphy, those present were asked "to consider the current and potential problems posed by the continuation of Murphy Delivery Service as a subsidiary of this corporation." One of the problems had to do with ICC regulations. Murphy told his fellow board members that he had received "legal advice from ICC counsel that the future plans of E. L. Murphy Trucking Company to expand and in such expansion acquire additional operating authorities were prejudiced by the continued ownership of Murphy Delivery Service, Inc."

Legal counsel, he explained, indicated that the ICC "has a well-defined policy against the holding of certificates in two separate entities

E. L. Murphy Sr., left, and
Dick Murphy with the double-
deck trailer Dick Murphy
designed in the 1950s to
haul golf carts manufactured
by the Toro Company.

under single control when the certificates held by each entity would permit, in whole or in part, the transportation of the same commodities between the same points." Furthermore, the better part of wisdom suggested that the trucking company's borrowing power "could best be applied toward E. L. Murphy Trucking Company's direct business and, perhaps, the Rigging Company, since it can generate business [for the companies] and substantial profits."

To set up Murphy Delivery as a separate entity, the directors authorized the borrowing of $100,000 from First Bank and directed the company attorney to find "suitable quarters" and personnel to handle its administration. Eventually, in 1983, Sears moved to another carrier and the delivery service "became a hollow shell," so Murphy closed it down. Ironically, some six months later Sears asked to return to the Murphy fold, but by that time all of the delivery trucks had been sold.

A Murphy Motor Freight truck in front of the state Capitol sports still another color scheme: light green on top, dark green on the bottom, with white lettering.

Needed: More Space

With their expansion in the 1960s, both E. L. Murphy Trucking Company and Murphy Motor Freight Lines, the larger of the two companies, needed more space. Ed Murphy bought property in Roseville for Murphy Motor Freight. The actual move to the new facility in 1965 came during typical Minnesota winter weather, a raging snowstorm. The following June, however, more than 2,000 people attended the grand opening of the $2 million Murphy Motor Freight Lines transportation center at 2323 Terminal Road in Roseville. The terminal, according to the June 29 edition of the *St. Paul Dispatch,* consisted of a two-level administration building, an 858-foot-long terminal building, a 20,000 square-foot maintenance building, and parking space for 700 units of equipment. "The terminal section," the newspaper noted, "is designed to handle five million pounds of freight every twenty-four hours for overnight delivery to 600 communities in the Murphy system."

Some years earlier, at its February 1, 1955, meeting, the E. L. Murphy Trucking Company board had approved the purchase of land in the Midway area for a new $125,000 office building and garage. "We wanted to move out of 1924 University Avenue because we needed a huge yard in which to park all the trailers," Dick Murphy explained. That $125,000 building never was built, however. In the meantime, he temporarily solved the problem by simply renting more space. In describing the move in her minutes, May Murphy revealed the growth of the company:

Murphy Motor Freight's then state-of-the-art terminal built in Roseville in 1967. At the time, the company was the largest Minnesota intrastate regular route carrier and its Roseville terminal the largest in the state.

During the summer [of 1957] it became evident that we were too crowded in our operating area at 1924 University Avenue. Accordingly, property was located at 2615 Wabash Avenue in St. Paul's Midway District which would permit of a combined operation. A lease was entered into with the Haldeman-Homme Co., owners of the property. The lease runs for (5) five years and calls for a monthly rental of $400. In order to serve our needs, a terminal building was constructed on the property. This building houses our central dispatching, drivers waiting room, and has a single stall repair shop. This was erected at a cost of $13,000.

Inside the Murphy Motor Freight Lines terminal in Roseville. At the center of this photo is the Terminal Control station where a supervisor monitored all the work that was being done on the floor below. In the rear of the photo is a motorized forklift that was used to move pallets of materials and goods around the floor and on and off the trailers that were parked next to the warehouse doors visible on the left and right sides of the building.

Ultimately, however, in the early 1960s Dick Murphy found a better location on County Road C, near Murphy Motor Freight's terminal, and E. L. Murphy Trucking would remain there until near the end of the 1960s. The two companies shared some facilities, including a computer center they set up in downtown St. Paul to bring the best available information technology to bear on their need for statistics. In an era when no one had heard of e-mail and cell phones, the Murphys' communications were sophisticated for the 1960s. WATS lines and a closed circuit Western Union Telex system linked headquarters with regional centers Dick Murphy was setting up around the country.

Murphy also had developed a complex, but highly effective, technique for managing his four companies. It was based on widely dispersed activity and delegation of authority and responsibility. He created a Control Office for each company, with one person in charge who reported directly to him. In turn, he dealt with each company only through its manager. He directed the administration of the companies from his headquarters in St. Paul with the help of computers and a corporate secretary. He also was a skilled "walk-around manager." He perfected the technique of unannounced visits to his several companies.

The regional centers he set up handled a diversified dispatch system that functioned in forty-eight states where E. L. Murphy Trucking Company had operating authority. The Western Regional Office was established in Los Angeles; the Central Office in Chicago; and the Eastern Office in Pennsylvania. Only the North Central Office was in St. Paul. A specialist there handled all the oversize and overweight permits from all states so that as a trucker moved across the country, the right permit was available at the right time for the right place. Murphy also created a coast-to-coast network of thirty-eight field offices that were attached to the regional offices and located in cities that were the company's key markets. Duluth, where Murphy trucks had been delivering for years, was the only such office in Minnesota. The major job of the field offices, Murphy told *Transportation Engineer* in 1969, was "to keep trucks loaded coming and going."

The equipment E. L. Murphy Trucking Company used in the 1960s to haul 60-foot-long prestressed concrete beams. The increasing use of such beams in the construction of buildings after World War II kept these Murphy trucks busy.

The dispatch operations' central control at Murphy Motor Freight Lines. Until the advent of computers, both E. L. Murphy Trucking and Murphy Motor Freight Lines tracked their tractors and trailers using the card system seen on the wall to the left of this photo.

The idea is that when a trucker from the Midwest arrives on the West Coast with his load, he'll find another load ready to haul back to the Midwest. Details of the delivery and pickup of that second load are handled by the regional offices or one of the dispatch offices. This was the "back haul" concept and I used leasing agents around the country to find loads.

"My job," he added, "was to see to it that the salesmen got the orders, that the company had the people and equipment to handle that business, and that the people and equipment were used properly to get the job done efficiently. My business philosophy always has been that nobody works for me. They work with me. My goal is to help them do their best."

At headquarters in St. Paul, he met every Monday of the year with the chief executive of each of the four companies. Every October those executives presented reports summarizing the work of their companies during the past year and their plans for the coming year. In November Murphy reviewed their reports. In December he spent a day with each executive, agreeing on the work for the coming year and assessing the resources that would be required. "That freed me," he explained, "to do the thinking and the planning needed to keep the companies growing."

By this time, E. L. Murphy Trucking Company had entered a new phase in motor truck operations. Unlike the early years of its history, E. L. Murphy Trucking Company itself now owned no tractors, the power unit that pulls the trailer. Instead the company contracted annually with the independent drivers, operators who owned their own tractors and hauled for Murphy in return for a share of the load at so-much per mile. The company did, however, own 225 to 230 trailers, most of them on air suspension systems. The company provided for their maintenance, and most of them were on the move continually around the country.

By this time, too, E. L. Murphy Sr., was less active in the business. He was beginning to withdraw. As Dick Murphy explained, "I tried to keep him in the loop, but he turned over the day-to-day operations as soon as he could."

He wanted me to run E. L. Murphy Trucking and he didn't want to interfere. He actually had very little to do with it during the last ten years of his life, and the more I got into interstate work, the less he cared about it. However, I always had an office for him. He'd come in every day around 10 o'clock, check the newspapers, come into my office if I was there, ask what was going on, check with the dispatchers, leave at noon, go home and take a nap.

Out with the window, in with the machine. E. L. Murphy Trucking had to take out a window to move in a big machine in the 1940s. The truck dates from the 1930s.

A side-by-side hauling operation by Murphy Rigging and Erecting in 1970. The man with the pole is holding up the electrical wires so the truck can pass underneath.

Doctors had warned the senior Murphy to change his lifestyle after his heart attacks in 1941 and 1942, and he followed their prescribed regimen religiously, napping and walking five miles a day almost until the day he died. There are family stories, however, that the father-son relationship did not always run smoothly, that the senior Murphy was a strict taskmaster. Dick Murphy recalled an early introduction to his father's approach to running a tight ship.

> That's when I first asked for a vacation. I was in charge of operations. We often worked Saturdays, and one Saturday we had to bring the vacation schedule into the meeting. In those days we got a week. When I got through the schedule, I said, "By the way, sir, (I always called him "sir"—it wasn't "Dad," it was "Yes sir, No sir") I've been here two or three years and I've never had a vacation. Would it be possible for me to have a vacation this summer? He looked at me—and I'll never forget it—and he said, "Answer me. Do you work Sundays? I said, "Well, once in awhile if something comes up." And he said, "You want a vacation? Damn it, you're working less than eleven months now. Next item." And that was the end of that. I didn't get a vacation. Not until sometime later.

However, he shruged off family stories about his father's testiness, his pattern of criticizing his son's management of the company.

I didn't pay much attention to that. I guess I was dealing with a man whose increasingly poor health was forcing him onto the sidelines. That must have been frustrating for him, although I didn't realize that at the time. I'd just go to work, he'd holler, I'd listen, I'd say "Yes sir, No sir." I loved my father and I always got along with him. I never noticed the criticism, never thought I should take umbrage at it. I knew he was a tough taskmaster, but I don't remember him doing anything to hinder my development of the company. He might have been extra hard on me to make sure I made it. That was part of my training. The company had to make money. By the 1960s the company really had taken off. We were expanding, and when we got out of the local cartage business, we started to make money.

As he neared the end of his life, Edward L. Murphy Sr., watched the inevitable transitions that were transforming the family-owned, family-run business he had nurtured for some fifty years. Ever since the 1930s, family members have recalled, almost everyone in the senior Murphy's family has had a role to play in the company. May Murphy

Murphy Warehouse Company's original building at 701 Twenty-fourth Avenue Southeast, Minneapolis. The main entrance was moved to the right after this picture was taken. Photo by Dick Palen, Edina, Minnesota.

An E. L. Murphy tractor trailer hauling a large steam boiler that has all its internal pipes exposed. A Murphy employee directs the driver. During transit, large wooden timbers, called cribbing, held the boiler in place on the trailer's flatbed.

had remained a company officer through the successful manuevers in the 1940s that brought Murphy Transfer and Murphy Motor Freight Lines back into the Murphy fold.

"In a sense," grandson Peter Maas has reflected, "her earlier career was almost a gold mine for her husband and herself because she had so many contacts; she knew how an organization had to be run. When she worked her way up at the Northern Pacific, she made sure she cultivated contacts at all stages in that orgnization. She must have been the most valuable secretary or personal assistant any railroad president ever had because she knew everyone. She was the first woman in that job and she had all those connections. "

In the late-1940s, with Dick Murphy ready to take over, her active role in E. L. Murphy Trucking came to an end, although she remained a member of the Murphy Companies' board of directors until she died in 1995. As Carole Faricy remembered it:

> I was still in high school at Visitation Convent when all of a sudden mother was home. She'd gone from being a business-woman, from marrying a man with five children and having two more children of her own, to going back to business, so she had no idea how to adjust to all this time at home. She really had a rough time there for awhile, but she got going. She played a lot of bridge, did a lot of volunteer work for Visita-

tion Convent where both Patty and I were students. She was a fine, self-taught, play-by-ear pianist and organist and she played the organ for services at the St. Paul Cathedral. She kept busy with us. She worked her way through it.

Peter Maas, now teaching physics at Strathclyde University in Glasgow, Scotland, remembered the Murphy household at 2020 Portland Avenue at about that time. The son of Genevieve Murphy Maas, the oldest of E. L. Murphy's seven children, Peter Maas and his sister Karen often spent childhood summers with the Murphys. In a way, he said, they were substitute parents because they spent so much time with them. His first memory of those visits dates back to around 1946 when he was six years old and traveled alone from his parents' home in Chicago to his grandparents' house in St. Paul.

A Murphy truck delivering a custom-made machine to a 3M plant.

I'd come up on the Chicago Northwestern with a "Put this kid off at such-and-such a station and hand him off to so-and-so" tag attached to me. For a little boy, it was like heaven on earth to travel on a railroad with only the train crew to look after you. I remember the brakeman teaching me the oil lamp signals to start and stop the train at towns along the way.

The house at 2020 Portland Avenue where the senior Murphys moved in the early 1940s. In the 1960s they moved to 740 River Drive.

Moving a kiln. One truck drives ahead, another backs up behind, as a man wearing a safety helmet signals the driver's turn.

He remembered his grandfather as "very dignified, with a fiery Irish temper. He once told me that 'I have the worst of both worlds. I have the temper of an Irishman and the stubbornness of a Dutchman.' When I imitated his swearing, I got my mouth washed out with soap, and that was fairly often."

> Business dominated the day-to-day, week-to-week life of the family. I can still picture my grandmother Murphy as running the house so smoothly you didn't know she was working, she so easily balanced her roles as working woman and wife. I was young, playing in the house and garden. Grandpa would come home for dinner like clockwork. She'd be cooking and I'd be allowed to sit at the kitchen table and have a glass of pop. I remember my grandmother as almost always at home, no longer working in the company's office. She had two teenage daughters to look after when I first started visiting there; she had grandchildren who were there often, and there were things to do with the grown-ups in the family.

As he grew older, Peter Maas learned something of his grandfather's work ethic. "He decided that it wasn't good for that grandson of his to be sitting around the house doing nothing, so he found something for me to do at the trucking company." Like Dick Murphy when he was young, Peter Maas "did a little of everything at the company's yard behind 1924 University where the front office was located."

> In the late 1950s I helped out in the paint shed, some in the office, but what was much more fun was being allowed in the

mechanics' area and being a pair of hands the mechanics could use on routine jobs. I loved being up to my elbows in grease and gasoline. One of my jobs was fueling the tractor rigs. The drivers would come in and pull up to the fuel stop. I'd refuel the tractors while they were checking in at the dispatch office. I was about eight or ten then and I did that almost every summer. I knew the engine shop and the paint shop, and anything else they could turn a kid loose on I got to do, from washing down the trailers to helping out in the spray painting and mechanics shops, sweeping out the garage and doing all the routine policing jobs.

An E. L. Murphy truck in front of 3M's building on St. Paul's East Side. 3M was one of the company's major customers.

He remembered walking to the University Avenue office with his grandfather each morning.

As he went through the yard, he'd drop me off wherever I was assigned to work, or he'd say, "Go find so-and-so." He'd go home for lunch but I'd pack my lunch and eat with whatever crew I was assigned to. Sometimes I'd eat at Porky's, the old drive-in a block east of the office. That was nice because behind it was a tiny park. I went back there long after the company had left the area. The park was totally overgrown with trees but an old Murphy trailer was still sitting there. Later, as a teen-ager, I worked as a forklift driver for Murphy Warehouse and as a dispatcher after the trucking company moved to its new location in Roseville.

Entrance to Murphy Motor Freight Line's office and terminal in Roseville.

Carole Faricy also remembered working at the company during those long-ago summers of the 1950s.

> If I didn't have a summer job, I worked there. I always did a lot of filing. Sometimes I washed some trucks, and I didn't mind that. It was kind of fun. The truck drivers were a riot. My father was really big in the garage, and it was fun to hear the banter. He'd yell at them and they'd yell at him, but nobody got vicious. It was still the old-fashioned hand-shake on a deal, a real level of trust among the guys.

She recalled the closeness in her family.

> There was a little sitting room between the bedrooms upstairs. Mother and Dad would sit there before dinner, have a drink, talk over their day, and perhaps work out some problems. I remember, too, that voting in elections was a big deal in my family. When we were old enough, mother and dad would take us out to dinner and then to the precinct where we voted. They made it a big occasion, a special thing. I did that with my children, too.

The senior Murphys eventually began to spend some winters in California and later on in Arizona. Carole Faricy remembered that:

Hauling 70-foot-long trusses. Photograph from the Kenneth M. Wright Studio, St. Paul.

When they first went out to California, they stayed at the Miramar hotel in Santa Monica. My Aunt Marge Downing, mother's sister, and her husband, Hyatt Downing, lived nearby and they had dinner with my parents every night. One year I drove out with them and I lived with Uncle Hyatt and Aunt Marge. He wrote westerns for 20th Century-Fox under the name of Hi Flood, and he got me a job as an errand girl at the studio. All I did was ride around on a bicycle, but it was wonderful. I got to see all those beautiful stars, like Gregory Peck.

In the mid-1960s, after selling their home at 2020 Portland, the senior Murphys moved to a newly-built high-rise apartment at 740 River Drive in the Highland Park neighborhood of St. Paul. He was struggling with declining health due to problems of undetermined origin. At one point he was scheduled for surgery to remove one of his eyes, thought to be the source of some of his problems. At 6 A.M. the day of the surgery, Carole Faricy walked into his hospital room to find him

A tractor trailer ready to transport a 85,000-pound rotary kiln. This photo was taken outside the E. L. Murphy Trucking Company office.

105

fully dressed. "I said, 'Dad, you're having surgery!' And he said, 'No, I'm not. I'm not having a good eye taken out. I don't care what it is, they're not taking my good eye.' And so they didn't, but eventually he started to go down hill."

He checked into the Mayo Clinic in Rochester, but doctors there were unable to identify the problem. Finally, however, he was diagnosed as suffering from a combination of leukemia and Hodgkins disease. Medication helped him live another few years. On August 9, 1969, at the age of eighty-one he died at home of pneumonia. His death certificate revealed that for the twenty-eight years since his first heart attack in 1941 he had suffered from arteriosclerotic heart disease.

His obituary described him as "a pioneer in the state's trucking industry." He was one of the founders of the Minnesota Motor Transport Association, and he belonged to the highly social St. Paul Club, which included some of his business cronies. Other memberships included the St. Paul Chamber of Commerce, the St. Paul Athletic Club, the Pool and Yacht Club and, as an active golfer, the Town and Country Club and the Midland Hills Golf Club. He served on several state commissions in the early days of highway development and had been a board member of the former Twin City Rapid Transit Company. Along with his son, Ed, who also served as a director of the Twin City Rapid Transit Company, his daughter, Carole, would in time follow him in a similar post with the Metropolitan Transit Company, the successor of what was once the Twin Cities' streetcar company.

4

The Fourth Generation Signs On

As HE DIRECTED THE GROWTH of the E. L. Murphy Trucking Company, Dick Murphy was traveling constantly, setting up agents, offices, and terminals in different communities nationwide. He became one of the pioneers in interstate heavy hauling and helped the industry's Minnesota carriers organize heavy-specialized divisions in states beyond Minnesota. Besides his presidency of Heavy Specialized Carriers of America, he was director of the Local Cartage National Conference (LCNC), a division of the American Trucking Association, and the Minnesota Transport Association's representative at the national level.

Dick Murphy and his new headquarters in Eagan, 1969.

With E. L. Murphy Trucking expanding, he watched its space needs stretch beyond the Roseville location where he had moved the company in the late 1960s. "We didn't need a lot of office space. The building could be relatively small—just a place for me and a small support staff. What we really needed far more was yard space where we could put trailers and tractors and move them in and out."

In 1968 Murphy leased six-and-a-half

107

acres of land from Bud Johnson, Inc., a Minneapolis firm that was developing the Sibley Terminal Industrial Park on Yankee Doodle Road in Eagan, the southern suburban area that lies between the Twin Cities. It was a fifteen-year lease with a purchase option. Murphy's plan was to build a new 7,000 square-foot corporate office building with a 10,000 square-foot shop, in addition to creating more parking for trucks. It turned out to be a complicated move. He also found that he had stumbled into history. Murphy vividly remembered a day late in June of 1968:

> We were out there on the Yankee Doodle Road property, preparing to officially break ground for the new facilities. Photographers were taking pictures. When I returned to our building in Roseville, there was a frantic phone call from the contractor. "Mr. Murphy," he said, "I think you'd better get back out here. We've just dug up a body." A skeleton had been uncovered. Archeologists from the Minnesota Historical Society were notified and all excavation was halted. They had uncovered an Indian burial mound. The property was on the highest point of land around there. The upshot was that we couldn't build on it, so we had to move.

Archeologists investigating the unearthed Indian burial ground in 1968.

It was a major find. The archeologists had determined that the hilltop site on the north side of Highway 13 and about three-and-a-half miles southwest of historic Fort Snelling was the sacred burial ground for some twenty members of Black Dog's village. A Dakota chief for whom the present-day power plant is named, Black Dog was the signer of at least two treaties between the European newcomers and the Indian tribes in the 1820s and early 1830s. He is thought to have died around 1834; the remains, archeologists estimated, dated from 1800 to 1825.

Researchers scraping dirt from bones and bone fragments and piecing them together found that the remains were lying in a row with their heads pointing in the same direction, unusual among Indian burial grounds. Also unusual for Indian burial grounds was that the remains seemed to have been buried in casket-like boxes, perhaps packing cases from the troops at Fort Snelling. A rifle ball was embedded in the shoulder of one skeleton, not surprising for a Dakota burial site at that time and place. Artifacts unearthed included beads, brass and china buttons, knives, gun flints, clay pipes, and, oddly enough, small purple lenses that might have been an early form of sun glasses.

As the excitement of discovery calmed down, Murphy leased five acres of nearby property from the Johnson company and after a nine-week delay, construction of the new offices and parking for trucks proceeded. The shop included two drive-through stalls, each of them long enough for two tractor-trailer rigs. The complex opened in April 1969.

Inside the Murphy Motor Freight Terminal in the 1970s.

In 1974 Murphy exercised the purchase option and bought the property for $189,812.

The new office building, one trade publication observed, "is probably the only trucking company office in the country done in Early American architecture and finished in salt-and-pepper brick. It might also be the only such office with a rug in tartan plaid on the floor of Dick Murphy's paneled office." Murphy has long exhibited a deft touch with promotion. He has had a hand in the designing and writing of any number of brochures for the company. A series of six brochures he developed with his vice president of marketing, Mary Boudreau, brought the company a first place award for Best Direct Mail Advertising Campaign from the American Trucking Association. He designed all the logos for the company, and they remain in use today.

Drawing on his Irish heritage, Murphy has used the color green throughout his companies, on his letterheads, his trucks, and other equipment. In addition, Murphy promotional materials have included drawings of a leprechaun nicknamed "Murph, " one of the mythical Irish "little people," and the words "Murphy Magic." Dick Murphy didn't limit the Irish theme to his businesses. His own green cars, green-rimmed eye glasses, green ties, and tailored suits with jackets lined in green satin, have made him and his company widely identifiable throughout the industry. So has his gift for the whimsical in marketing. There is a company story that, peeling off his jacket at a special event, Murphy revealed its green lining, then began tossing out dozens of white baseballs with green lettering. With his children, Richard and Maureen Murphy Aro, he designed the familiar logo of a crane for Murphy Rigging.

As the E. L. Murphy Trucking Company moved into the 1970s, a series of well-calibrated successes, as well as some challenging changes,

SEVEN YEARS OLD AND IN A MURPHY TRUCK

My first recollection of the Murphy Motor Freight Lines dates back to around 1946-47 when I was seven years old and chasing parts in a 1941 Ford service truck with Art DeYoung, our legendary maintenance man. We were still in our old terminal on Broadway in the Lowertown district of St. Paul. By the time I was ten, we had moved to a new terminal at 965 Eustis in the Midway area. This was a state-of-the-art facility with an overhead drag line used for LTL shipments. I still reported to Art DeYoung every summer. Art put me in charge of cleaning up and stocking the parts room. After awhile I was promoted to assistant janitor.

I remember Joe Kalal, an old-time mechanic with several missing digits, who would take me home from work each day. Joe always carried a black metal lunch pail to work. Pretty soon I was carrying one too (age twelve), just to be like the real mechanics. Each day at noon the shop would come to a stop as the mechanics set a plywood sheet on two sawhorses, ate lunch, and played nickel/dime poker. I was a keen observer.

As the years went by, I moved from the shop to

the dock where I learned the freight business from Mike Flaherty. Mike always seemed to save the loads of "farm jewelry" for me. He was one of the old breed; if you were not producing, Mike would say "Get a move on; all you ever think about is home and pay day!" During this period, I also worked for Vernon "Red" Kirsch on "Red's Crew"—a band of young expendables who did maintenance around the property. I distinctly remember reroofing the Eustis terminal in July 1958—a hot, dirty job, for sure. And all the while Red would be giving his crew the needle about "having to drive a stake in the ground to see if we were moving."

During college I became a city driver each summer, reporting to Dan Greenberg. Business was booming. We built a new terminal in Roseville in 1965. This was at the time of the great 1965 flood. I vividly recall April of 1965, sandbagging and manning pumps with Red in order to keep water out of the brand new terminal office. Still in law school, I worked summers as a dock foreman. During this period we made a major acquisition, expanding our route structure east of Chicago

accompanied the sixty-six-year-old company into its next decade. Over at Murphy Motor Freight, Ed Murphy followed a widespread business trend of those years and took the Freight Lines public in 1972. At E. L. Murphy Trucking, Dick Murphy did not, preferring to keep his company private as he pursued his long-time interest in heavy hauling and in nurturing the warehouse arm of the company.

The move to Yankee Doodle Road in 1969 had been among Dick Murphy's expansion plans for a company that was basking in the affluent years of the trucking industry. Murphy Rigging and Erecting, a business that grew during the 1970s, handled the more exotic assignments. In 1973 the company took second place honors in a national trade competition for moving four gigantic adapter rings for a radar installment at Nekoma, North Dakota. Rigging had hauled four of the rings 900 miles from Sturgeon Bay, Wisconsin, and the fifth ring the 525 miles from the Twin Cities. Nearly thirteen feet high

through the industrial heartland of America to Buffalo, New York. We were doubling in size every five years, and we went public in 1972.

After military service and finishing up at the University of Pennsylvania's Wharton School of Finance and Commerce, I returned to work full-time in 1971. I learned much from "Skeets" Becker, vice president of operations—another icon. I became director of Line Haul Operations, then served as a regional operations manager with ten terminals, including Chicago.

The acquisitions continued with the middle states in 1975, giving us more density in Indiana and Ohio. I assumed major sales responsibility in 1976 until the untimely death of John Summers, vice president for sales. He was a former World War II marine, a role model and a mentor. In 1978 I became vice president of sales and operations, then executive vice president when "Skeets" retired. That year probably was the high water mark for the Freight Lines, with a revenue of $75 million, profit of $2.6 million, and a 93.2 operating ratio. I became president of Murphy Motor Freight in June, 1980. I was thirty-nine. Then deregulation

hit. From this point forward, we struggled and eventually succumbed in 1987. I had left the company in 1986.

I joined Honeywell that April, and was assigned to Building Control Products. I was on my own, as a Business Unit Director, in a 100-year-old high tech company that was one of the Dow Jones 50. At that time Honeywell had a revenue of about $6 billion and operated world-wide. I retired from Honeywell in 2001 when the company merged with Allied Signal. I was fifty-eight. By that time Honeywell had grown to $25 billion. During my fifteen-year Honeywell career, I traveled globally, finding my niche in Building Services, one of Honeywell's most profitable businesses. While there I had a once-in-a-lifetime business success by being part of a business team that created from scratch in eight years a $1 billion worldwide business internally in Performance Contracting. I left Honeywell as director, Distributed Power Generation, Building Solutions and Service Division.

Edward L. "Mike" Murphy III

E. L. Murphy Trucking Company team working in Hudson, Wisconsin, in the late 1970s. Left to right; Darrell Smock, Ron Gunderson, Jay Hassett, Jim Hanson, and Charlie Timp.

when boosted onto the truck, each ring was thirty-two and a half feet wide and weighed 98,000 pounds. They traveled at night so as not to block traffic on narrow country roads.

In Minneapolis Murphy Rigging hoisted two ninety-eight-ton cable supports 180 feet to the top of the new Federal Reserve building and anchored them in place with bolts almost eight inches in diameter. The company also moved into place a huge 125-foot-long kiln at Anchor Block Company. Almost thirteen feet in diameter, the kiln weighed around 130,000 pounds. The riggers used two trucks and many twelve-by-twelve-foot beams to slide the kiln through a partially completed wall. In another operation, a seventy-foot manufacturing tower weighing 180,000 pounds was hauled to a site several miles outside of Duluth.

In January 1980 Murphy Rigging moved a Milwaukee Road dining car from near the state Capitol along University Avenue to Rice Street and out Rice to County Road B-2 where it became the Roseville Crossing Restaurant. It required two tractors hauling two lowboys

'FIVE DOLLARS AN HOUR'

I started working for the Murphy Warehouse Company in 1975 as customer service manager for the cigarette warehouse office. I was paid $5 an hour. At that time, all the wholesalers in town got their cigarettes from Murphy, and they still do, although sales have dropped 30 percent from what they were twenty-five years ago. So many people have stopped smoking. Manufacturers used to ship cigarettes to the warehouse by boxcar and truck. But then thieves began to break into boxcars in the rail switchyards. Now, because of security concerns and transit time, cigarettes are hauled entirely by truck.

In 1979 I became operations manager for the entire company, and I've watched it change dramatically throughout the past two decades. At first there was little employee turnover, but we began to grow in the 1980s. Our personnel has tripled in numbers. We used to have three warehouses around the Twin Cities. Now we have nine and almost two million square feet of space.

Most of our people work in the operations department because we're a service company. We own and operate all our own trucks, trailers, and equipment. All of our people, even our drivers, are company employees. We have an interchangeable work force. One day a person will be driving a truck; the next day he'll be stacking pallets in the warehouse. By moving workers around, we give our people a variety of jobs to do. When work is slow in one area, we can move people to another area where there is greater demand for them. In other companies, if there isn't a load for a driver to haul, that person doesn't work. Today we operate all over Minnesota and parts of Iowa and Wisconsin with our fleet. For our U.S. distribution products, we rely on our contract carriers.

Paul Welna, vice president of operations, Murphy Warehouse Company.

Aerial view of Murphy Warehouse Company, as it looked in 1972. The Minneapolis skyline is off to the right.

moving side by side and taking up all four lanes on Rice Street. They moved by night. Pat Sullivan, who began work for Murphy Rigging in 1972, remembered getting up to watch it. "It had to be at night."

The company moved entire manufacturing plants, large machines, and printing presses. They erected temporary housing. They once moved an elephant, with disatrous results. As Dick Murphy remembered it, there was a circus in St. Paul and for some reason the Republicans wanted an elephant brought up to the Capitol.

> So I sent a truck, they loaded the elephant into it, and the elephant unloaded pretty heavily while it was being transported. To get the smell out we had to take out the floor of the trailer and replace it.

Using both cranes and their riggers, Murphy Rigging hoisted the weather ball to the top of the former Northwestern National Bank building in downtown Minneapolis and later took it down again. In

113

WAREHOUSING OPERATIONS HAVE CHANGED

Over the past thirty years, warehousing operations have really changed a lot and the Murphy operations have had to keep pace with these changes. Today trucks are bigger, wider, higher, and they can haul more goods than in the past. At the same time, Murphy warehousing operations also depend on rail shipping. One boxcar can hold the same volume of goods as three trucks can carry. The trade-off for this increased volume, of course, is that it takes longer to ship the same distance by rail than it does by truck.

We're probably the largest warehouse company outside of Chicago. At the same time, our customers today are more demanding in the services we provide to them. In the past, 70 percent of our orders were known the day before their scheduled ship dates. Today, in contrast, many of our orders are shipped the same day we receive them from the customer.

One of the reasons for this is that customers want their goods delivered sooner than in the past so that they can keep smaller inventories. When they can do this, they have less capital tied up in their inventories. Over the past few years, our industry has grown more complicated, and the work pace has speeded up substantially. To meet the demands of this faster pace, we've bought more

equipment and found ways to increase the productivity of our workforce.

As customers have changed their ways of doing business, such as maintaining smaller inventories, we've changed our way of doing business to keep up with them. One aspect of our relationship with our customers is that we have very few contracts with any of them. Although some warehouse companies operate only with written contracts, we have accounts that have been with us for thirty years without needing this type of arrangement to work together. I think this speaks well for our company.

In some cases, we've been able to turn potential industry disadvantages into advantages. Thus the warehouses we built in the 1990s are bigger than many older facilities. They have indoor rail tracks to facilitate loading and unloading without regard to the outside weather. The lighting in these facilities is better, and they were designed to provide plenty of wide-open space for the easy movement of goods on forklifts.

Valuable as these improvements are, the most important services that we offer to our customers today are security and sanitation. In the area of security, our warehouse operations are run so that the computerized inventories of our customers are pro-

1990 they hauled down Midwest Federal's Green Tree sign from its building in St. Paul. They moved a railroad caboose, sculptures for artists, and MRI machines. Murphy remembered that,

> When they were new, we moved MRI machines into St. Joseph's Hospital and several other area hospitals. We kept hauling bigger and bigger things; as machines grew in capability, they also grew in size, complexity, and delicacy. That was our stock in trade. We couldn't just throw something on a truck. We had to be careful, but we moved those machines and other heavy equipment like that all around the Upper Midwest area and eventually all over the country.

tected against any outside interference and their products are held in secure facilities at all times. Every day we conduct an inventory count to make sure that we do have what the customer expects us to have. In addition use of a variety of security procedures, such as the requirement that employees wear identification badges to ensure that only authorized personnel have access to our warehouses, the use of TV cameras for constant video monitoring of warehouse floors, the regular use of random patrols by our security personnel, and mandatory driver check in upon arrival, all provide a high level of security at all times.

Sanitation also is a high priority in our operations because that's part of what our customers require in a warehousing operation. In all our facilities we employ an outside, independent company that inspects our sanitation systems and procedures twice a month and certifies that we are in compliance with all industry standards in the area of sanitation.

Another strength of our warehousing operations is our minimal turnover of truck drivers. Most are long-term employees. In addition we have our own maintenance and repair staff. Because we don't outsource these services, our maintenance staff members know the repair history of each piece of equipment and its necessary maintenance cy-

cles, and they have the tools and workspace to make repairs on site. If the repairs can't be made on site, then they can haul the equipment to our central maintenance shop.

In terms of equipment, the forklifts we used in the warehouse really changed in the 1980s and 1990s. Initially the freight was hand-piled and hand-loaded. Forklifts used to weigh 6,000 pounds and lift 3,000 pounds; now forklifts weigh 10,000 pounds and lift 6,000 pounds. Ray Svoboda remembers that it took six men to unload each Westinghouse freezer from a railroad car. With OSHA's strict standards, the forklifts' engines are cleaner burning; they can do more work and lift twice as much; they are easier and safer to operate, and more user-friendly for the operators. They now have ergonomic seats and seat belts, as required by OSHA.

One of our warehouses is paperless. Customers input the order information into the computer system. All of our warehouses have locator systems. We have to keep track of each line in each load in case there is a recall.

A simple product that has changed the warehouse industry is shrink-wrap. It prevents damage and keeps products stable while in transit or in storage.

Paul Welna

Pat Sullivan remembered that, "In the old days, crews built cribs board by board all the way to the top of the machines they were moving, then took the cribs down piece by piece when the move was completed. They didn't have the big gantries and cranes they do now."

"The Rigging business is feast or famine," Dick Murphy once said. "We can work eight-to-twelve-hour days or as long as the project lasts." Today the work flow is somewhat more predictable as Murphy Rigging and Erecting has evolved into a millwright/rigging contractor that specializes in machinery moving and erecting, millwright services, plant set-ups and relocations, maintenance, heavy lifts, specialized transportation, and handling delicate art and medical pieces.

KEVIN SHIELY MURPHY AND THE FREIGHT LINES

I graduated in 1975 from the University of St. Thomas but it would be five years before I joined my brothers in Murphy Motor Freight Lines. With a BA in accounting, I went to work first for the St. Paul CPA firm of Taylor, McCaskill and Co. I began like all grunt, aspiring CPAs by working long hours for low pay on audit teams of various sizes. This experience, however, brought me into contact with some of Minnesota's great corporations and nonprofits: Donovan Companies, Andersen Corporation, Blandin Paper Company, and the Minnesota Chapter of the American Red Cross, to name just a few.

It was an invaluable time in my career.

In the fall of 1980, my brother Edward L. (Mike) Murphy III, then president of Murphy Motor Freight Lines, Inc (MMFL) asked me to join the internal audit staff there and I did. This allowed me to work under Frank Black, senior internal auditor and legendary thirty-year veteran of the company. Frank had a photographic memory of every company policy, as well as those of the DOT, ICC, and a host of other governmental agencies. He was well respected within the company and I learned a great deal from him as I began my financial and operating education in the LTL industry.

This was not the first time I'd worked for MMFL. During summer vacations in high school from the late 1960s to the mid-1970s, I had worked on the maintenance crew and in the parts department at company headquarters in Roseville, as well as in the accounting department in the Hamm building in downtown St. Paul. This brought me into contact with some of MMFL's

unique personalities, such as Vernon "Red" Kirsch, Marv Lindquist, Tony Jones, John "the Rammer" Ramsey, and Patricia Wagner, among others.

I learned the most from Red Kirsch. I swept trailers, cleaned toilets, painted everything standing still, welded, cleaned the drag line, cleaned the scale pits, and worked the non-stop trash details. At age fourteen, I learned from Red how to drive a manual transmission. Red believed there was no commercial cleanser that was effective for the nasty cleaning jobs at MMFL, so he brewed his own concoction that was as secret as the Coca-Cola formula. But what I learned most from Red was to show up, work hard, and be accountable. That has stayed with me throughout my life.

In 1982 I began to move through a variety of financial roles in MMFL, including internal auditor, financial analyst for operations, assistant treasurer, and treasurer. This brought me under the tutelage of Herman Selz, who had been the financial genius of the company since joining it right out of service in World War II. In 1984, Herman retired and I was chosen to replace him as vice president, finance, and chief financial officer. I was thirty-one years old. I hoped I could fill Herman's big shoes.

I remained in that position until MMFL ceased operations in February 1987. From 1987 to 1995, I worked for Michael Foods, Inc., in Minneapolis. Since 1996 I have been the principal of Antietam Creek Solutions, LLC, providing contract management for founders of development-stage companies.

Clients range from industrial manufacturers and printers to medical and high technology firms to artists and military units responsible for classified equipment.

Tim Lyons, now Senior Project Manager for Murphy Rigging, has seen many changes throughout the past decade or so as Murphy Rigging evolved into the business it is today. The most important changes, according to Lyons, have been the increasing emphasis on operating safely and more professionalism among riggers. Forklifts are larger, heavier, and have more lift capacity. Hence Murphy Rigging's purchase of the Versa lift, the first in this area, with its 60,000-pound capacity and extendable counterweight

The dolly systems have changed from steel wheels that tore up the floor of a facility to the new neoprene wheels that leave the floor intact. For some projects, Murphy riggers even use air dollies that carry the load on a cushion of air so that the equipment to be moved never touches the floor. Murphy Rigging has two sets of hydraulic gantry systems that can lift up to 400,000 pounds. Although the candlestick gantry system is still in use, the new hydraulic systems are the preferred technology. Similarly chains and nylon ropes have replaced pulleys, ropes, hooks, and stacks of tires. Hydraulic power has also replaced brute force applied through muscle power. OSHA today has strict tagging rules for all lifting apparatuses. "We still use wood and steel pipe rollers," Lyons said, "and cribbing, made with the type of wood railroads use for their ties."

Rigging today is a mixture of science, art, and experience. A rigging handbook of weights and measures is available, but most of the men working for Murphy Rigging today have learned the business from their fathers, brothers, or uncles. "We've employed many father-son and brother teams over the years," Dick Murphy remembered. "We've had Liggetts, Johnsons, Dibbles, and Gluzes." Today a "Vo-Tech program offers the rigging basics, but mostly it's still on-the-job training."

"It takes a certain type of person to be a rigger," Tim Lyons observed. "They must have excellent mechanical ability and good physical coordination. They must be able to think independently, make quick decisions, and be flexible and open to change. It is hard physical labor; it calls for the development of good techniques and a sense of 'feel,' the 'art' part of the profession."

Riggers are Department of Transportation certified drivers, subject to random drug testing. They also function as customer service representatives. "Many of our customers ask for their favorite rigger," Lyons said. "Riggers know customers want their machines moved with care. All our moves are sensitive and involve expensive pieces of equipment. Damage can mean down time for customers, especially if the equipment is one-of-a-kind. Much of our rigging work involves repeat customers. Riggers pride themselves on doing it right the first time. Each move is complicated. First we have to figure out how to do it; then we have the challenge of doing it."

BRIAN MURPHY: 'A GOOD LEARNING EXPERIENCE' AT MMFL

My first memory of Murphy Motor Freight Lines was as a child when my father would take the entire family over to the Murphy terminal at 965 Eustis Street on Sundays. That would have been around 1962. I remember the kind of art deco look to the office, the stairway from the first floor up to the second floor, the green, black, and gray flooring, and most of all the ten-key adding machines on the desks of the people in the office.

I remember my Dad's office with the window that overlooked the yard, dock, and maintenance areas. I remember distinctly the move to 2323 Terminal Drive in the spring of 1965. The run-off from that year's snow and rain caused a flood that threatened the not-yet-opened office, terminal, and maintenance areas. There was a crew (my brother Mike was part of it) organized by Red Kirsch that was sandbagging and using pumps to keep the water at bay. Their efforts worked, and the buildings weren't damaged by the flooding.

A few weeks later the grand opening of the terminal took place and I remember how big the dock was, compared with the old building. The dock has a "Towveyer" system in the floor that towed carts around the dock. On this opening day the kids were allowed to ride on those carts to their hearts' content.

I had worked at MMFL during the summer months of 1967 to 1973 when I was in grade school and high school. I was assigned to Red's crew, a maintenance crew led by Red Kirsch who was responsible for all building, mechanical, and yard maintenance. Tom Brown supervised me. My summer jobs were painting garbage cans, sweeping out trailers, painting garbage cans, fixing the wheels on the freight cars, painting garbage cans, pulling nails from trailer floors, and any other jobs Red saw fit to assign.

During college (1974 to 1977) I graduated to running parts for Tony Jones in the Parts Depart-

ment. This meant trips to Mack Truck, Boyer Ford, Power Brake, and various other suppliers. I also remember a trip to pick up a case of "sky hooks" at some supplier on University Avenue. This was a trick the mechanics liked to play on the new guy and they all had a good laugh when I returned. I remember some of those mechanics: Larry Guzzo, Gary Stone, Joe Kalal Jr., Dick Martin, Jimmy Ketchell, Duke Stegmeier, to name a few. All great people!

After graduating from St. Louis University in St. Louis, Missouri, in 1977, I started at MMFL full-time. My first assignment was as a sales rep at the St. Paul terminal. I worked for Neil Engquist, sales manager in St. Paul. The St. Paul sales staff was a veteran group. They included Kenny Basma, Don Johnson, Larry Barnacle, and Steve Kelly. After about a year I was transferred to the sales department in our Omaha, Nebraska, freight service center where I covered Omaha and the surrounding areas. Selling freight was not my strong suit, but it was a good learning experience for later life. In the spring of 1980 I moved back to St. Paul to work as a dock supervisor. Dick Grathen was terminal manager, and Steve Mudge was dock manager. I worked all three shifts over a period of twenty months.

In 1982 I was transferred to our Line Haul operations area, working at the MMFL offices in the Hamm building in downtown St. Paul. Angelo Perez was Line Haul manager, and I worked evening hours from 3 p.m. until midnight setting up the dispatches of our eastern Line Haul operations. I was promoted to Line Haul manager in 1984. The following year, 1985, I became assistant terminal manager at the St. Paul Terminal. Later that year I was named terminal manager, a position I remained in until MMFL ceased operations in February 1987. After MMFL closed, I worked for Sinclair & Valentine Ink Company in 1987 and 1988 as a transportation manager. In 1989 I took a position with Musicland Corporation as director of transportation. In 2002 I moved into a similar position with Regis Corporation in Minneapolis, where I remain today.

Working on the dock and involvement with the St. Paul operation allowed me great experiences that I still draw upon today. There were great people there: Dick Lorvick, Max Durand, John Korlath, Caeser Ketchell, Red Kirsch, Bill Gear, Val Carlson, John Ramsey, John Ray, Tom DeRusha, Ken Olsen, Marv Lundquist, Marv Witte, Ken Overfield, Tony Jones, Dave Webb, Dick Eaton, Bill Bresse, Pat Mantalica, Loretta Steinke, Andy Wolf, Jeff DeYoung, Skip Hoven, Mary Lou Tucker, Jim Babel, Ray Mescke, Ed Said, Jim Gabler, Jim Stewart, John VanArsdale, Sandy Johnson, again to mention just a few. All were long-term employees and were typical of the people who made Murphy Motor Freight Lines what it was.

I was there at the end when the company shut down. It was obviously a difficult time for the company, our family, and our more than 1,000 employees. A message was sent to all terminals and freight service centers at about 1 A.M. on February 24, 1987, advising all locations that the company was ceasing operation effective immediately. As terminal manager in St. Paul, I delivered the news to our employees as they came to work or came in off the road from their evening runs. The response was one of shock and disbelief, but no anger that I saw. They knew the company was having financial troubles but they believed we would continue to operate and they always would have jobs.

All those who still were working for MMFL at the end were for the most part long-term employees with some twenty years with the company. They all had a hand in building it from a small Midwest operation to a major LTL carrier that served a large portion of the eastern half of the country. It was an orderly shut-down, which was characteristic of the company. Freight was picked up at our terminals by American Freight for delivery to customers, and equipment was marshaled to be sent to selected sites for auction.

I remember that the news of the closing of the company was on the front page of the St. Paul Pioneer Press. WCCO radio led its hourly news with the report and stories appeared on each local newscast in the Twin Cities. The articles, news reports, and editorials generally put the company in a favorable light. One editorial stated that the company had been "deregulated to death." Most reports talked about what a great corporate citizen the company had been for the Twin Cities and Minnesota over the years of its existence.

The knowledge I gained during the time I worked for MMFL was invaluable. By the age of thirty-two, I already had experienced things other people in the industry may never encounter. The total experience, good and bad, is one I never would trade. I cherish the time I had to work with my father and brothers at this great company.

"We try to be partners with our customers," Richard Murphy Jr., said. "Most of them are well-trained engineers who design the machines we move. Sometimes we reengineer the planned move to fit our scope of the operation." According to Tim Lyons, "The customer does the paperwork, but we provide the reality. That reality can mean bracing and reinforcing a floor three stories down to move a MRI medical device through a hospital lobby."

The rigging business today is still heavy hauling, moving medical equipment, printing presses, breweries, food plants, generators, and transformers. It also includes plant maintenance as well as providing services at equipment auctions, handling plant relocations, providing optic leveling, doing security business, and moving artwork. "We'll bid on anything," Lyons said. It's a far more sophisticated process today, but not unlike, perhaps, Murphy Transfer's heavy hauling almost a century ago.

A Variety of Jobs

With its work for the federal government's Department of Transportation and for companies throughout the United States that had government contracts, Murphy Trucking often moved highly sensitive, highly secured cargo. Murphy described the process:

> We'd park a trailer at a facility, then take the tractor and crew away, leaving the trailer behind. The drivers never knew what was on the trailers because the company would load them and call us when the load was ready to go. We'd come with our tarpaulins, cover the trailer, haul it out, then park it in an area the customer designated and leave. The customer's crew would unload the trailer and call us when the trailer was back on the tractor. We'd bring it back here. Boeing, Federal Cartridge, 3M, FMC all had federal contracts and E. L. Murphy did the hauling for them. Those were the sorts of loads that made the business exciting.

Whenever possible, tractor, trailer, and crew would travel at night. When over-dimension permits based on width, height, or length were involved, the permits would dictate whether a load should by hauled by daylight, or at night. Dick Murphy explained:

> Our drivers also couldn't travel during rush hours because they didn't have permits giving them permission to do so. If

The 1984 Nation's Capitol Christmas Tree leaves the Minnesota State Capitol. Dick Murphy, far left; Mary Boudreau in dark coat; Richard Murphy, second from right.

they came to a city at 3 o'clock in the afternoon, they'd have to park outside until 7 at night. If it was getting dark, they wouldn't be able to move again until the next morning. And there were restrictions as to the number of hours they could drive without stopping.

One move involved a submarine built by General Electric. As John Solum remembered it,

> We had to take it to the East Coast and we had Secret Service people front and back. The cargo was kept wrapped so security

Dick Murphy with driver Alvin Hauck and Mary Boudreau, vice president of communications for E. L. Murphy Trucking, as the Christmas Tree was on its way.

Hauling the Nation's Capitol Christmas Tree out of Minnesota's Nemadji State Forest in preparation for the tree's trip to Washington, D. C. in 1977.

wasn't compromised. Another interesting move was that twelve-foot aluminum tank we drove to Texas for the beginning of the space program.

Then there was the Nation's Capitol Christmas Tree, a fifty-two-foot white spruce that E. L. Murphy Trucking Company volunteered to haul to Washington, D. C., in 1977. It was a massively complicated operation. When the National Capitol Christmas Tree tradition began in 1964, trees were selected from farmland around Washington, and later from national forests. In 1977, for the first time, a Minnesota state agency was asked to provide the tree.

The majestic, perfectly-shaped white spruce started life as a seedling in Nemadji State Forest near Nickerson in Pine County around 1917. Sixty years later it was due to be harvested for timber. Instead, it ended its life as a glittering Christmas tree. Dick Murphy selected Alvin Hauck, Murphy Trucking's Driver of the Year in 1976, to take the tree to Washington. It wasn't easy. The huge tree stood deep in the forest beside an old logger's trail. Both the trail and a wide area around the tree had to be cleared to create passage for Hauck's tractor, a forty-foot flatbed trailer, and a twenty-ton crane.

When the tree was cut in November of that year, the temperature was far below zero. It was hauled first to a nursery to be warmed until its limbs were supple enough to allow bending, binding, and wrapping, and its twenty-eight-foot diameter reduced to eight-and-half feet. Picking up his 1,800-pound load, Hauck then headed for the nation's capital. On his way, Hauck and officials from the state forestry department and the Murphy Company called on six elementary schools in suburban St. Paul, where 800 school children saw the tree and heard its story.

Send-off ceremonies at the state Capitol launched the trip east, a 1,300-mile route along highways that required special over-dimensional permits negotiated by the trucking company. The trailer was plastered with signs announcing its cargo as "The Nation's Capitol Christmas Tree from the Forests of Minnesota" and inviting passers-by to "Watch me light up on December 14." Arriving in Washington on December 5, and under police escort, Hauck drove to the Capitol grounds where the tree was cemented into a hole five feet deep and its wrappings and bindings loosened. The United States Marine Band played, and workers perched on scaffolding began to hang 4,500 white, clear, blue, and amber lights, and 5,000 ornaments. Back in Minnesota the following spring, the clearing where the great white spruce had stood and the road reaching it were seeded with clover to provide habitat for wildlife.

Office of Murphy Rigging and Erecting, Roseville, late 1970s and 1980s.

In 1984 E. L. Murphy Trucking again donated its services to haul the Nation's Capitol Christmas Tree from Superior National Forest, near Tofte, Minnesota, to Washington. Driven by another member of the Murphy Company's Driver Hall of Fame, David E. Knobloch of La Crosse, Wisconsin, a tractor-trailer bearing the seventy-five-year-old, sixty-foot-tall white spruce set off from St. Paul on November 27 for

Murphy Rigging and Erecting Company placing the lions on the steps at the Minneapolis Institute of Arts.

Removable gooseneck trailer moving a transformer base unloaded from a ship.

Washington. On December 12 the tree, with its lights and ornaments, was presented to the nation.

Hauck and Knobloch were typical of many of the contract truckers who began driving for E. L. Murphy Trucking Company in the 1960s and 1970s. They were independent operators who owned their own tractors or power units, but usually used the company's trailers. The rise of the independent operators was not new to the trucking industry. As Dick Murphy observed, "Before the First World War, a trucking company often started with a man who had a team of strong horses, a wagon, and a customer with a load to be hauled. That's how my grandfather began." In the 1920s, to meet the postwar demand for goods, those independent truckers hired more drivers, bought more trucks, and formed companies. Their ability to haul caught the railroads by surprise and set off fierce competition for freight. When E. L. Murphy Trucking was founded in 1936, the company owned its own trucks and trailers and hired its own drivers, all of whom belonged to the Teamsters' Union. Regular, full-time employees were paid by the hour under a contract that also provided benefits.

At the end of World War II, the earlier pattern repeated itself. Again, it was driven by the mushrooming need for motor carriers to handle the massive demands, pent up during the depression and the war years, for goods of all kinds. Consumers, businesses old and new, manufacturing plants, other freight-generators, and again the railroads scrambled to keep up with the demand. There were acres and acres of new houses needing stoves and refrigerators and sinks and bathtubs. Faced with such opportunity, a returning veteran with a truck or two found it easy to appear on the scene as an independent operator. Murphy remembered that,

> A friend of mine, Harold Anderson, came home from the navy, started driving a truck for a mill outside of St. Cloud, and Anderson Trucking grew from there. Other men came home from service, bought their own trucks and just started hauling. After being in the army, a lot of men wanted to be their own boss. They'd learned how to run trucks and repair them.

By this time trucks were far more reliable too. They had proved that by their use during the war years; they had shown that they were capable of traveling cross-country, rather than just locally. Before the war, Murphy recalled,

> If we hauled as far as Rochester, we'd have to carry a mechanic with us. I remember as a kid riding in the trucks to Duluth at night during the summers. The driver would have a tool box with him and many a night the truck would quit.

A Murphy Rigging crew installing a generator after hauling it to the site. The crew will also handle maintenance after the generator is installed.

Murphy Rigging moving a Nordberg generator in the late 1970s.

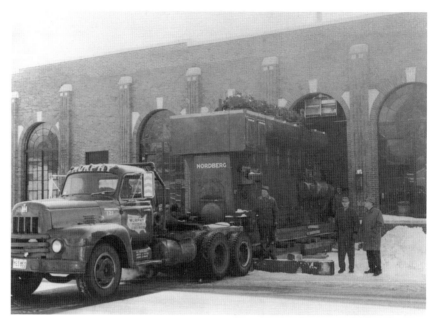

We'd pull off to the side of the road, throw up the hood, figure out the problem, fix it, and keep on going.

E. L. Murphy Trucking had begun to hire independent drivers like Alvin Hauck with his power unit in the 1960s. The company would provide the trailer, do the sales work, and assemble the load. Looking back, Dick Murphy believes that the growing use of the independents was a major factor in changing his company's entire culture. It enabled E. L. Murphy Trucking to develop into an interstate freight-hauling company, rather than remaining a local Minnesota cartage operation. It allowed Murphy to compete with such major users of this system as International Transport, a postwar company out of Rochester, and C&H Transportation out of Dallas. Both grew into behemoths.

Making Their Own

As Dick Murphy observed, "It was in our best interest, of course, for drivers to own their own power units. We didn't have to make the investment in the unit, and that's the heavy expense in a tractor-trailer. We subcontracted with them. That all changed, however, in 1971. With the signing of a new union contract between Local 120 of the International Brotherhood of Teamsters, the contract drivers became employees of the company and thus were entitled to benefits.

Murphy Trucking bought most of its equipment from trailer manufacturers. However, the nature of the heavy hauling business and the amount of business the company was doing with such clients as 3M re-

Murphy Warehouse Company employees in 1989. Left to right, front: Sue Oslund, Jackie Nihart, Joyce McMaster, and Barbara Nihart. Standing in back are Michael Good, left; Paul Stevens, Dick Baker, and Bob Doerr.

quired them to make some of their own trailers at the Roseville plant. "As 3M expanded their facilities, we became their fair-haired carrier," Murphy recalled. "Much of the growth in the trucking industry that required those huge trucks came about during the 1970s."

> Those trucks really weren't that big in today's terms, but they were fifty-to-seventy-ton capacity trailers and that was huge for that time. Since we were hauling heavy, bulky stuff, we used low-boys, which were the heavier capacity units, and flat-beds, which were flat—forty-eight to fifty-two inches off the ground, and the workhorses of the trade. A low-boy comes back from the tractor, drops down, runs to the rear, and frequently goes up a bit over the wheels. Low-boys have heavy beams that allow them to handle far heavier commodities. That's where we got our leg up on the competition that didn't have that. We built some of our low-boys in our own shops. Others we'd buy when we got enough money.

Ron Gunderson, who joined Murphy Trucking in 1969 as an operations trainee and rose to the vice presidency for operations, remembered the 1970s too:

> We had different types of trailers for different loads: step-deck double drops for high loads and removable goose-neck trailers. As we got more and more into the specialized loads we needed multiple axle rigs—nine axle and twelve axle. It was a specialized area, but the rates were very high. We had to get special permits. Then we found that the drivers needed some big horsepower rigs with four axles. It was a learning experience for all of us, but it was worth it. It was very lucrative. When the company opened an office in Hudson, Wisconsin, I was put in charge, and that became our hiring office. The rates

Murphy Rigging moving a coiler or generator on two removable gooseneck trailers.

for Workers' Compensation were much cheaper in Wisconsin and our contribution was much less. The late '70s and early '80s were our best years, with a peak of around $33 million.

The combination of those huge rigs and the wide, well-kept roads of the expanding interstate highway system linking major cities permitted companies like E. L. Murphy to move their operations beyond their states and regions and into the national and international arena. The special hauling authority to do that, Gunderson remembered, meant that companies needed to apply to the federal Department of Transportation for authorization to enter a certain state or region.

"In order to acquire that authority," Gunderson said, "Murphy would buy a company that had the authority where the company needed it. For example, Murphy bought Dyer Transportation, based in the Northwest, so Murphy Trucking could do business in Oregon. They bought Crown Transport, a company in Pennsylvania." As Dick Murphy explained:

> I bought authority along with Crown and put that authority together with the authority we already had to allow us to operate from Minnesota and the Midwest to the East Coast and back. We had to buy Crown to get the rights to operate from here to the East Coast.

Gunderson remembered that "Companies had gateways. If we originated a load in Virginia, we had to touch base in Minnesota before we could go on to the West Coast. We had tariff books that looked like

128

encyclopedias and listed every piece of equipment by number and rate. It was confusing. Later it was based on how much of a trailer you were going to use and how many miles you were going to travel."

By the 1970s, the trucking industry had grown far more complex than it had been during the earlier years that John Solum recalled:

> In 1946 when I was a dispatcher for E. L. Murphy, the dispatcher gave out the assignments, picked the drivers, and assigned the rigs. We had a board on which we listed all the assignments, the drivers, and when they were to show up for work the next day. It was my job to write up the assignments and give each driver his written ticket. The jobs were assigned by seniority.

But as the years wore on, changes were inevitable, some of them industry-wide. Dick Murphy pioneered the use of husband-and-wife partnerships in driving the huge trucks for Murphy Trucking. "When they put power steering on the trucks and power brakes on the power units, a woman could handle a truck as easily as a man," he observed. "They could spell each other and speed up the driving. Of course, we had to pay for the second position, but we insisted that they not take children in the vehicles."

The major change, however—the serious, devastating change in trucking—arrived during the Carter administration late in the 1970s as the federal government moved to deregulate the entire transportation industry. Back in 1925 when Minnesota introduced its early attempt to control the chaos that had entered the infant trucking industry, the cut-throat competition by the independent operators of that day threatened to undercut the established operators and upset the industry's economics. The result was Minnesota's requirement that truckers apply to the Minnesota Railroad and Warehouse Commission for certificates permitting them to carry freight from point to point. Ten years later in 1935 when the federal government's Motor Carrier Act placed buses and trucks engaged in interstate commerce under the authority of the Interstate Commerce Commission, the ICC licensed all routes. Carriers applied for certificates that were needed for each trip and rates were uniform for all routes. It was the official birth of the regulated trucking industry, as Ryan Murphy, Ed Murphy's grandson, observed in a 1996 paper, "The Devastation of Deregulation," which he wrote for his class in Minnesota history at Macalester College in St. Paul. His study traced the "transforming effect" of deregulation on both the trucking industry and the Teamsters Union.

How do they get around in the warehouse? Dick Murphy took this photo of Bob Doerr (left) and Dick Baker with Dick's new bike in the mid-1990s.

While the Motor Carrier Act of 1935 was a New Deal effort to level the playing field for truckers struggling through the Great Depression, the 1980 Motor Carrier Act had its origins in the Great Society programs of the 1960s and the creation of the federal Department of Transportation. "The Motor Carrier Act began," Ryan Murphy wrote, "as a bipartisan Congressional effort to reduce shipping costs, increase the productivity of the transportation business, stimulate industrial growth, and counter the inflation and economic stagnation that set in after 1970."

The OPEC-generated oil embargo of the early 1970s, he noted, also played havoc with the American economy. Transportation costs shot up; labor alone accounted for 65 percent of the cost of shipping a truckload of freight; fuel costs also spiraled upward, from 14 cents to more than $1 a gallon.

It was a frightening period, especially for those who all too clearly

Military hauling on a single-drop trailer by E. L. Murphy Trucking Company.

remembered the Great Depression. Moreover, it followed on the heels of the prosperous 1950s and 1960s—decades of massive growth for the motor carriers as the hauling of freight moved from railroads to trucks and airplanes.

The 1980 act, perhaps unwittingly, initiated an almost eerie repeat of those barely regulated 1920s as it opened the doors to anyone who had the money to buy a truck and rent a place to park it. The upstarts were free to slash rates, and did. Deadheading—a return trip without a load—would become a huge trial for truckers to bear. Ron Gunderson recalled that,

> A lot of independent truckers got into the business when the industry was deregulated. For instance, a farmer from North Dakota who had a couple of trucks for hauling his grain to market would decide to pick up a load so he didn't have to return with an empty truck. That's how it worked with deregulation. But Murphy Trucking was a union carrier and we had work rules that tied our hands and prevented us from being flexible. If you had a load in a given area, you had to go down the line and offer it to the first person on the list until you found someone to take the job. They had a right to pass it up because you didn't employ them. That meant we didn't have the flexibility to change as the industry changed.

As Ryan Murphy pointed out, the trucking industry always had been a boom-and-bust cyclical industry. Truckers had survived wars, recessions, depressions, oil crises, foul weather, and lawsuits stemming

Murphy Motor Freight's new terminal in Roseville, which opened in 1967. Exterior brick is green!

THE TOPSY-TURVY 1980S AND '90S

When I joined the Murphy Companies in 1977, I worked at the E. L. Murphy Trucking offices in Eagan as controller for all the companies. During that time, Dick Murphy saw that I'd taken an interest in warehousing, so in mid-1979 he offered me the opportunity to move to the Murphy Warehouse Company.

In 1982 I left to go to work for Space Center, a local competitor, but after two-and-a-half years there, R. T. hired me back. That's one of the things he used to do. He always left the door open for people to come back—people who perhaps had decided the grass was greener on the other side of the fence until they saw all the brown patches. So he kept the door open. A lot of employers wouldn't do that.

The country was facing major problems around 1980. Interest rates at close to 20 percent limited the ways in which the Murphy Companies could expand by either leasing or buying property. On top of that was deregulation. Not only was deregulation devastating for the trucking industry, but there was a section in the regulations called the Winn-Dixie amendment. It was promoted by, and thus named for, the supermarket chain that served the East and South. Under this amendment, the trucking companies were by-passed and grocery stores, for the first time, were allowed to come into the warehouses to pick up their freight. This had a big impact on our trucking operations.

Prior to 1980, we received a lot of products by rail. It wasn't unusual to get twenty or thirty boxcars of toilet tissue and napkins from just one source. However, deregulation and the decision to allow trailers to have a new maximum length of up to fifty-three feet made trucks competitive with rail delivery, especially on shipments that had to travel under 1,000 miles.

The Just-in-Time (JIT) concept, which reduced inventories, and the uncertain economy had a major, destructive effect on both the warehouse business and the trucking companies. After all, if the trucks weren't hauling freight, they weren't putting it into the warehouses, either. Through skillful management, we weathered the uncertain '80s and early '90s and we had only a voluntary layoff in the '90s. Then business rebounded.

Even though our volume of business was improving, we had to remain flexible and innovative, both as individuals and as a company. On Thanksgiving Day 1990, for example, we all lost a close associate in the company when Bob Eginton passed away. Our loss of Bob meant that I had to take on more of a sales role for the company. Similarly in the late 1970s and early '80s, we had been buying used equipment for the warehouse, but in the latter part of the 1980s, we started purchasing more new equipment, which benefited our operations by paying dividends in increased productivity that just wasn't possible with used equipment.

Another illustration of how our warehousing operations had to be ready to change came unexpectedly in mid-1993. The Burlington Northern Railroad asked us if we could set up a warehousing operation to handle rolls of paper from the Blandin paper mill in Grand Rapids, Minnesota. About the same time, the Onan Corporation in the Twin Cities needed warehousing space for the generators they built. Although the availability of warehousing space for lease was tight just then, we were able to work out a short-term lease for the former Quebecor building in Fridley. Coincidentally, the Burlington Northern had rail tracks, which were essential for paper deliveries from the mill, to the Quebecor facility and it owned a nice piece of land on the other side of the tracks.

At the same time, the cost of leasing industrial

132

real estate was going up; thus ownership began to make more fiscal sense than leasing did. So in 1994 Murphy Warehousing bought part of the adjacent land from the railroad and built Northtown I on the property, thereby replacing the Quebecor facility. This decision resulted in a large, new warehouse with ten indoor rail spots. Many people aren't aware that printing is Minnesota's second largest industry and the printers in our state have the fourth largest printing capacity in the U.S. Thus our paper warehousing operations have continued to grow since the mid-1990s because out-of-state paper mills have chosen to send us paper for storage and delivery to Minnesota printers.

When we negotiated the initial land purchase from the railroad, we also asked them to put a hold on selling the remaining property for our possible future expansion, "in five years or so." By 1997 we had bought this land and built Northtown II.

Onan's requirements for warehousing of their generators, however, needed a comprehensive solution. So in 1999 Murphy Warehouse built Northtown III on Onan's campus. We share the space with Onan and have good rail access to both U.S. and Canadian rail lines. Here we were able to consolidate all of Onan's outside warehousing in one building, but this new facility also gave us space in which we could expand our transload capabilities for the panel board, shingle, and bulk food industries.

At the same time that Murphy Warehouse was building these new facilities, the industry was moving to longer-term agreements in contract warehousing for the beverage, fulfillment, industrial equipment, and pallet rental services. The terms in these agreements could be for providing labor only, or services on a cost-plus basis, or for full management services. Whatever the terms, both parties saw them providing greater cost stability than the older,

thirty-day arrangements that were typical in public warehousing.

Another unexpected problem that Murphy Warehousing was able to solve in the late 1990s was the Y2K scare. When we designed our computer operating system for the warehouse in 1979, no one gave any thought to the year 2000 because the expectation was that in the next twenty years the initial system would be replaced. It wasn't, and it couldn't handle the century change. Once we became aware that this was a major problem that we had to solve, a committee of six managers and staffers reviewed a number of possible new systems and made a recommendation for purchasing a new operating system. Beginning in July 1999, those involved in the installation of this new computer software spent many long and stressful hours making sure that everything in the new system functioned properly prior to the end of the year.

Today Murphy employees continue to work hard to retain the loyalty of their customers. They strive to adapt to the changing circumstances of the warehousing industry whether they come from federal regulations that affect safety, national security, or working hours and conditions, or from broader economic circumstances, such as the globalization of the marketplace and international trade conditions, or from more rigorous service standards demanded by our customers. In addition we have taken the initiative to improve our level of service through our decision to seek certification through the ISO Quality Program, increased safety training, and a willingness to seek continuous improvement in our operations and productivity.

Mike Butchert, senior vice president of sales, Murphy Warehouse Company

from accidents. It is little wonder that the companies of the 1970s, particularly the mid-sized operations, believed they could survive the upheaval brought on by yet another spell of deregulation. But for too many it was not to be. Too many forces at the national level were battering the industry.

With the surge of inflation during the 1970s and early 1980s, the Department of Defense began to slash orders for equipment, eroding the need for truck deliveries. The recession of the 1980s devastated the country's industrial sector and trucking companies watched with dismay as their tonnage dropped precipitously. Profit margins within the industry shriveled. The Teamsters Union suffered too. Although trucking companies had been strongholds for union labor around the country, the union also representated a bureaucratic force that was almost impervious to change. The National Master Freight Agreement (NMFA), engineered by Jimmy Hoffa and his International Brotherhood of Teamsters in 1964, spelled out pay policies for drivers, pay rates, hours worked, benefits, and pensions. Companies that failed to sign on found picket lines outside their doors. Finally, Ryan Murphy wrote, the advent of deregulation proved to be an insurmountable barrier for many regionally centered, unionized, family truck lines, like the Murphys' that had been founded decades earlier. The figures revealed the disaster: In 1978, the eve of deregulation, 162 companies filed for bankruptcy; in 1985, only seven years later, there were 1,533 bankruptcies, and a similar number for each year throughout the rest of the 1980s.

An End of an Era

At E. L. Murphy Trucking Company out on Yankee Doodle Road, matters came to a head in the mid-1980s as Dick Murphy fought the debilitating forces of deregulation. He remembered that the trucking industry was almost totally deregulated by the early 1980s:

> By then it was open season. Anybody could get into the business and charge any rate they could get. Trucking industry earnings just plummeted. When they started going down, I figured this is ridiculous, and if we keep at this, we'll go broke.

Murphy Rigging's dead-of-night moving of a Milwaukee Railroad dining car from its site a mile from the St. Paul Waterworks. On its new site at 2295 Rice Street, the rail car became a restaurant.

It was a complicated combination of circumstances. The nation was in a recession and trucking companies all over the country were bleeding financially. Another factor was that the insurance industry was in turmoil. While union negotiations were going on, bad news arrived at the Murphy company. Carriers Insurance of Iowa had been taken over by the state and forced into bankruptcy; 2,000 carriers had to shut down. While E. L. Murphy Trucking could still get insurance, the cost was prohibitive. Added to this, for Murphy Trucking, were problems with the Teamsters Union, "a long accumulation of problems," Dick Murphy recalled, "that had been created by constant union attempts to interfere with our plans for the company at a time when the Twin Cities was a strong labor market."

> Drivers for the original company, E. L. Murphy Trucking, and for Rigging and Erecting, were union members when my father was alive, and we knew we couldn't change that. When the hauling end of the business began to expand, we could see that's where our big growth would be.

When non-union independent drivers began to pour into the industry, Murphy wanted to hire them. "We were competing with those non-union companies and that's when I worked out an agreement with Local 120 that allowed me to use the independent contractors."

> I promised the union that I would not eliminate any of the existing drivers who were on the seniority list and I would not

hire any new drivers. In short, I would protect the drivers who already were there. As business increased, we hired more and more of the independents. We paid them a percentage of the line haul revenue—so much a mile, as opposed to the earlier system that was based on an hourly rate with benefits. The impact on our payroll was huge. On the other hand, many of our drivers were still union members, and that made it almost impossible to compete with non-union companies.

All might have been well for a time, had Murphy's arrangement with Local 120 remained in place. He had argued that the agreement allowing the company to use independent drivers for over-the-road hauling "kept the union teamsters busy as long as we could bring equipment in and out of the city. I wanted to be able to feed those people, and the union went along with me on that."

By the 1980s, however, union pressure to organize the non-union drivers was unremitting, stemming, in part, from the union's own struggle to maintain its position nationally as a stronghold of union power. The Motor Carrier Act of 1980, in its zeal to control costs, had dealt a massive blow to the transportation industry, their insurance carriers, and also to the unions associated with the industry. Dick Murphy resisted efforts to unionize all of the company's drivers.

> I finally ended up with a sort of quasi-contract that allowed the company to continue to use the independent drivers, but the people who handled the loading and unloading had to be union. We'd been growing at a good rate until the union moved to organize the whole place. Our interstate heavy hauling was non-union and we couldn't survive under the union terms and conditions. The union called a strike. I arrived at work one morning in 1985, and there were pickets out front.

Murphy issued the following statement:

> E. L. Murphy Trucking Company was notified by Local 120, IBT, of the commence of a strike on December 3, 1985. Picket signs have been posted and a number of contractors [truck drivers] have participated in the strike action. The Company has continued to offier dispatch, many of which were refused or delayed. Obviously, operations cannot continue on this basis. As a result, the Company hereby gives notice that those contractors continuing to participate in the strike or refusing dispatch will be permanently replaced. . . . The Company deeply regrets the circumstances which have led to the current situation. During the lengthy bargaining, the Company

disclosed in great detail the serious economic conditions which exist. The Company repreatedly expressed its belief that the last offer represented the maximum which could provide a basis for the Company's continued operation.

On December 18, 1985, he called together the people in the office and told them he was shutting the door. "I said we'd sell everything here, and I'd concentrate on the warehouse and the rigging business." It was an emotional decision for him; he was seeing his lifelong dream go out the window. It was devastating. "Still, I'm proud that I made it. I really had no option. I had built E. L. Trucking into one of the major heavy haulers in the nation, but I knew that in the long run I had to close it down." The state and national trends of the past fifteen years that had ensnared the family business also had created the need for Murphy to make the inevitable transition from trucking to warehousing and distribution, following the national trend from manufacturing to a service industry.

He vividly remembers the company's last days. "Our lawyer guided us through the intricacies of shutting down a company. He said, 'Announce your shutdown, then wait for the dust to settle and see who's left.'" On December 27, 1985, Dick Murphy's announcement went out to all E. L. Murphy Trucking Company contractors:

> It is with the greatest reluctance that we must inform you that E. L. Murphy Trucking Company is permanently ceasing operations effective immediately. E. L. Murphy has been insured by Carriers Insurance Company of Des Moines, Iowa. As most of you are probably aware, Carriers has been forced into rehabilitation and has cancelled our insurance coverage effective January 1, 1986. Despite our best efforts, we have not been able to obtain replacement insurance coverage at a price that the company will be able to pay. Thus, we are unable to comply with federal and state insurance requirements and are obliged to immediately discontinue operations as a carrier.

"When a company closes," Murphy said, "people begin to leave, but that didn't happen to us. There was great sadness and there were tears, but hardly anyone left. They stayed to help us close down. It wasn't just a matter of jobs for them or money or benefits, all those things tied up in their working lives. It was a matter of caring, of their sense of pride and ownership, of their own identity being tied up in the company. It was incredible for me to see that."

His daughter Laurie Murphy remembered her grandmother's dismay. May Murphy had worked hard beside her husband to help E. L.

Murphy Trucking prosper and she still served on its board. "I said, 'Grandma, if you'll look at the books, you'll see that the money just isn't there. Our only option is to shut down.' She was shocked. She couldn't believe it. But then she repeated what might well be the Murphy mantra: 'Well, you know, we always survive.'" The trucking company's properties were sold in a nationwide auction that netted more than $3 million.

Two years later, the end also arrived for Murphy Motor Freight Lines. Although it was not organized and incorporated until 1930, Murphy Motor Freight could trace its ancestry back seventy-four years to 1913 and the incorporation of its parent, Murphy Transfer Company. While Edward L. Murphy Sr., had lost control of the company during the depression years of the 1930s, he and his son had brought it back into the Murphy fold in 1945. For the next forty years, Murphy Motor Freight did well, but by the 1980s, with the upstart non-union carriers cutting rates right and left, the company was struggling to stay afloat. Throughout the industry, cost-cutting seemed the way to solvency.

"Capital investment decreased dramatically," Ryan Murphy wrote. "Old tractors were rebuilt instead of retired. Management was downsized. Unprofitable routes to outlying areas were dropped." Nothing seemed to work. The Teamsters' Union came under attack too, he noted, "as the federal government 'busted' teamster domination by undermining the ability of the unionized sector of the economy to exist."

Ed Murphy realized that his people were becoming "fundamentally disoriented," not understanding what was going on, scared and apprehensive, wondering if they would have a job tomorrow. It was a

Dick Murphy and his mother, May McGinnis Murphy, touring the warehouse in 1991.

death watch. The lawyers arrived in February of 1986. Ed Murphy re-called the reasons behind the anguished parting:

> The motor carrier industry was built by hundreds of family-owned enterprises at a time when Teamster Union labor dominated the trucking industry's labor force throughout the country, except in the South. Deregulation in 1980, with free-dom of entry, ended the Teamsters' power over the system. It was devastating to the pioneer carriers who had been saddled with the National Freight Labor Agreement, a device that made it almost impossible for individual companies to re-negotiate their contracts with their truckers. The playing field was no longer level.

While deregulation's impact on the trucking industry was devastat-ing, Ed Murphy said, it also was a direct attack on organized labor, the companies' largest cost. As he observed:

> The Teamsters refused to recognize that their power was gone, that the impact on thousands of motor carrier workers with good jobs would be fatal. For Murphy Motor Freight, a well-run organization, revenues at its peak averaged $85 million annually, with 1,500 well-paying jobs, but as the industry dis-integrated, those jobs were lost. . . . So one afternoon we went down to the Minnesota Mutual building in St. Paul. And we decided. Shut her down. After midnight, down she goes. We went to work the next morning and it was nothing but tears.

When Dick Murphy shut down E. L. Murphy Trucking Company in 1985 and when the trucks stopped rolling at Murphy Motor Freight's massive terminal in Roseville, an era ended for the Murphy family. It also ended for all of those men and women who had worked for the two companies.

By the early 1980s, however, the fourth generation of Murphys had begun to join the family firms. At Murphy Motor Freight Lines, Ed-ward L. Murphy III, known as "Mike," already had succeeded his fa-ther as president of Murphy Motor Freight Lines in 1970, and his brothers, Kevin and Brian, also had gone to work for the company. In 1982 Laurie Murphy, the oldest of Dick and Helen Murphy's five chil-dren, joined E. L. Murphy Trucking. She was followed in 1983 by her brother, Richard Murphy Jr., known within the family, the company, and out in the business community as "Richard" to distinguish him from his father.

Murphy

May McGinnis, of St. Paul went home to God in her 99th year on Oc-tober 27. Born in Ra-cine, Wisconsin, she was preceded in death by her husband, Edward L. Murphy, Sr. and Gene-vieve Murphy Maas.

She is survived by Ed-ward L. Murphy, Jr. (Mercedes), Dorothie M. Fellows (Gray), Althea M. Nelson, Richard T. Mur-phy, Sr. (Helen), Carole M. Faricy (Richard), Pa-tricia M. Millard (George), by her grand-children: Peter Maas, Karen Althea Maas, Ed-ward L. Murphy, III, Shawne M. Monahan, Tara M. Varco, Brenna Murphy, Megan Murphy, Kevin S. Murphy, Brian Murphy, Lynn Nelson Bisanz, James L. Nelson, Jr., Laurel May Murphy, Richard T. Murphy, Jr., Patrick D. Murphy, Shar-on M. Garber, Maureen M. Aro, Althea Clare Faricy, Bridget Nyhan Faricy, Ben H. Millard, G. David Millard, Ste-phan G. Millard, Megan Murphy Millard, by 33 great grandchildren and 2 great, great grandchil-dren, and her devoted caretakers: Bert Klabun-der, Carol Hovda & Paula Adamson.

MAYDEAR will long be remembered by all her family and by her many friends. She was loved by and was an inspira-tion to all who knew her. An early business woman in St. Paul, she was one of the first women to be the private secretary to the presi-dent of a major US rail-road. She co-founded E.L. Murphy Trucking Co. in 1936 with her husband. Working side by side with him, she helped build the firm in-to a nationwide motor carrier while creating a loving home for the growing family. She was long active in the Guild of Catholic Women, the Home of the Good Shepherd, Visitation Convent and St. Thomas Academy Mother's Clubs and the St. Mark's Par-ish Fortnightly.

Visitation is one hour before the Mass of Christian Burial at the Church of the Nativity, Prior & Stanford Ave-nues, St. Paul at 10:00 AM on Monday, October 30. Private interment at Calvary Cemetery.

No flowers, please. Me-morials preferred to the Marian Center or to the charity of the donor's choice.

Arrangements by O'Hal-loran & Murphy, 575 South Snelling Avenue, St. Paul, MN

May Murphy's 1995 obituary in the October 29th edition of the St. Paul Pioneer Press.

'EARN YOUR WAY . . .'

"I told my children when they were growing up that I would never ask them to join me in the business, but if they made a decision to do so, and asked to come to work here, they're not as the boss's son or daughter, but as an employee who has to stand on his or her own merits. I had to take that position in fairness to the other people who had committed their lives to this company."

Richard T. Murphy Sr.

Both Richard and Laurie Murphy had realized early on that their futures lay with the company. Richard Murphy : "The company was always there, off on the horizon. Although it was a family business, it was never pushed on us, which I really appreciated."

For Laurie Murphy: "When I was fifteen, I decided I wanted to go into the family business. My father always has been one of my mentors, and I wanted to follow in his footsteps."

Both of them, following family tradition, had worked for the company after school, during weekends, holidays, and summers as they grew up. As Richard described it,

> I remember the old terminal near the intersection of Highway 280 and University, but by the time I was a freshman or sophomore in high school, the terminal had moved to County Road C. I remember painting parts bins there with a friend from St. Thomas during Easter break. I remember cutting grass at the Eagan property during the summer. I remember deciding where the trees should be planted there.

Laurie Murphy worked at Murphy Warehouse during the summer months.

> I did clerical work. I worked in the traffic department and the customer service department. I did filing and sales work, and I did consolidations. That meant making up truckloads for the various points where we were delivering. I made up bills of lading. I delivered paperwork from building to building. I marked my way through the warehouse—turn left at Cream of Wheat. We wore little gold smocks so we didn't get our clothes dirty.

Both "interned" elsewhere before joining the family business. Richard feels strongly about this.

> From my own experience, I think it is extremely important to work somewhere else for several years, to grow up in that process, to know what it's like not to have your name on the door or the building. I learned that you must earn your respect every day, especially if you're a family member. After I graduated from college, I went to work for the Walter Butler Engineering firm of St. Paul, one of the original builders of the state Capitol.

140

Inside a Murphy Warehouse dock, with railcars on either side. In this facility eight railcars can be unloaded at the same time.

After college, Laurie Murphy worked for B. Dalton Booksellers in Minneapolis for ten years.

> But I'd gone as far as I could there. I wasn't being challenged. It was a business that I knew, that was easy for me, but I've never regretted leaving it. I just wanted to be a strong team player. The family business seemed to offer that challenge.

The company Richard and Laurie Murphy entered in the 1980s was still the E. L. Murphy Trucking Company where both worked their way through the shop. Richard Murphy was assigned first to Dispatch.

> Then I moved on to Central Control and then to sales for the Twin Cities region. After that I was placed in charge of international sales, but that was a long, slow process, and the trucking company shut down soon afterwards, so I wasn't with the trucking side of the business for very long.

Laurie Murphy came into the company as an assistant in marketing.

> I worked directly with our marketing director, Mary Boudreau. I did sales bonus calculations, new market research, maps for sales meetings. Before we liquidated the trucking company, I also was on a training program Dad let me develop for myself.

I spent three weeks in licensing, three weeks in Dispatch, and three weeks in Operations. I spent a full year working on the liquidation, and eventually I became our first Human Resources person for the warehouse.

Both completed graduate degrees from the Carlson School of Management at the University of Minnesota, Richard in 1986 and Laurie in 1989.

With the demise of the trucking company, Dick Murphy turned his attention to the company's other major assets, the Murphy Warehouse Company and Murphy Rigging and Erecting. After its spin-off from E. L. Murphy Trucking as a separate corporation, Rigging had continued to function well for some twenty years under the Murphy banner. Then there was the warehouse. Dick Murphy looked back on its history:

> Back in 1952 the trucking company had authorized the sale and transfer of $3,928 in equipment to the warehouse company, but it wasn't formally incorporated until October 10, 1956. The first warehouse I had was in an old storage building at University and Snelling avenues. I used to wash our trucks there as a teenager, and that's where the Twin City Rapid Transit Company had kept parts and supplies. They had emptied it, so I rented it, and that's where Murphy Warehouse Company had its first warehousing operation.

E. L. Murphy Trucking was in the local cartage business then, but Dick Murphy had long had an eye on the warehouse business in general and its potential for the growth of Murphy Warehouse in particular. He was well aware of the success of St. Paul's McNeely family with their St. Paul Terminal (separated now into Space Center and Meritex), the

---

ADAPTING TO THE 1990s

When I started here in 1977, the warehouse was a small operation. We did things on a shoestring. We simply made do. In the 1980s it made sense to lease, rather than own real estate. We generated business with the railroads, who said they needed a warehouse for paper. So we found an old, empty building where TV Guide once was printed, and we set up there.

When we received goods on pallets, we'd replace that pallet with another that was not usually of the same quality. We'd check out the pallets and send them out for repair, if necessary. It's a separate operation, which we still do. It wasn't until late 1989 that the warehouse company really took off.

Mike Butchert

Morse Company in Minneapolis with their Security Warehouse, and Pratts Express, a rigging company that hauled heavy machinery.

> We'd also been hauling machinery to warehouses around the country and it just occurred to me, why don't we do that? I saw people in the warehouse business who'd become multi-millionaires and I figured it would be a good business to get into.

Warehousing, of course, was not a new venture for the Murphys. In the 1920s, after the Murphys changed the company's name to Murphy Transfer and Storage Company, they built the two warehouses, one in Minneapolis in 1923 and another in St. Paul in 1927, to store goods they hauled between the two cities. Both warehouses were lost to American Bank and its voting trust in 1935, but E. L. Murphy Trucking continued to perform warehouse functions in that old storage building at University and Snelling.

At first, bread-and-butter for the warehouse, Dick Murphy remembered, was the Seeger Refrigerator Company on Arcade Street in St. Paul. His father had begun hauling for Seeger back in the 1930s when Seeger was making refrigerator cabinets only and needed a place to store them. Dick Murphy, however, remembered that by the time he got involved with the Seeger business, Seeger had become the Seeger-Sunbeam Company and was putting Sunbeam units into the cabinets.

> They came off the assembly line as complete units. After Seeger-Sunbeam was acquired by the Whirlpool Company in Benton Harbor, Michigan, we continued to run the warehouse for Whirlpool. We'd pick up the units at their plant on Arcade Street and ship them out by truck or rail.

The warehouse operation began to grow. John Solum recalled that once Seeger had a lot of aluminum gasoline tanks and needed a place to put them.

> We stored them in a place where Mr. Murphy said they used to keep the horses. The tanks were wing tanks for airplanes. Then forklifts came in. The first of the forklifts had a 1,000-pound capability, and those lifts grew and grew in size until they had a 2,000-pound capacity. That made it possible for trucks to do work they couldn't have handled in earlier years. The Toro Company was another customer and we also did a lot of grocery and food business.

A Murphy Rigging gantry lifting a hydraulic punch press. Mike Bennett, shown here, was one of the crew.

Then, as Dick Murphy concentrated on building E. L. Murphy Trucking's heavy specialized hauling operation during the 1950s and 1960s, the warehouse "just went along," he said. In years to come it would prove to be the future for the Murphys. When he began to expand the operation, he joined the American Warehouse Assoociation, contracting with two or three warehouse sales entities that had people working in New York, Chicago, and on the West Coast. Their calls on warehouses soliciting business for the company provided Murphy with his first outreach:

> I backed that up myself by traveling to some of the major cities where I had other interests and where I knew of some firms that might have warehouse business for us.

Those trips for the warehouse proved to be an education for him, too. As he saw his trucks hauling more and more machinery and other bulky items to and from a growing number of sites around the country, he decided "we'd better stay in the warehousing business:"

> My father didn't agree. He was very happy to remain in local cartage. He didn't want to do anything to disturb the cash flow from the E. L. Murphy Company. He had done well in E. L. Murphy Trucking. It really had taken off after World War II.

In 1972 Dick Murphy bought the property that the warehouse still occupies on Twenty-fourth Avenue in the Midway district of southeast Minneapolis. He had been renting it and other locations "as needed" from Alex Tankenoff and his Hillcrest Development Company.

Originally the site of the Wabash Screen Door Company, the property was "out in the country" and Wabash's owners preferred office buildings in downtown Minneapolis rather than suburban locations. As Murphy tells the story:

> The site already had a number of older, multiple-storage buildings on it. After we moved in, Alex said, "What you need is a larger facility, and we're prepared to build it for you but we want a long-term lease." We made a deal with him, and he built the first part of this facility. When the lease was up, he said, "Dick, you need to own your own facility." So I borrowed some money from the bank for the down payment and bought it. Our oldest building on the south came first. Then we built to the north.

In 1966 the warehouse company completed a 105,000 square-foot building. Six years later another major expansion added another 180,000 square feet to the complex, and before that year was out, still another 335,000 square feet of space, giving the warehouse a total of

"Class photo" from 1969. Dick Murphy and John Solum at the top. Some are still here, some have retired.

MURPHY WAREHOUSE COMPANY
MINNEAPOLIS, MINNESOTA

NOVEMBER   1969

680,000 square feet in all of the company's facilities on that site. The entire complex, which today houses the Murphy Warehouse Company, Murphy Rigging and Erecting, and the Murphy Companies' corporate offices, is now the Murphy Industrial Park.

An International Arena

Three years after the shutdown of E. L. Murphy Trucking Company, the first in a series of milestones for the Murphys brought the Murphy Warehouse operation into the international arena. In 1987 it became the first public warehouse in the region to function as a Foreign Trade Zone. Created at the federal level in 1934, Foreign Trade Zones only took off as a tool with a U.S. Customs Service ruling in 1980 that eliminated the "island" model and the assessment of duty on U.S. value-added activities, Dick Murphy said.

> We were expanding the warehouse business and doing a lot of work with such local companies as 3M and Honeywell that were developing products overseas. These companies were bringing goods in here from overseas and taking goods manufactured here and shipping them back overseas. We saw that we could become the intermediary.

Dick Murphy described the company's entry into this new federal program. Since a government agency, rather than a private company, must actually hold the Foreign Trade Zone license, the company first approached the Greater Metropolitan Foreign Trade Zone Commission, consisting at that time of the cities of Bloomington, Minneapolis, and St. Paul. He learned that the Commission was seeking a site. "We convinced the Commission that we were an existing company with existing facilities already providing services to the transportation industry, which really is what a Foreign Trade Zone should be, and the Commission decided to license us to operate on the Commission's behalf."

Technically, Dick Murphy explained, wherever a Foreign Trade Zone is located, the property is international, not American. That means that goods shipped to a Foreign Trade Zone have not yet actually entered the United States. Companies are permitted to hold merchandise in a Foreign Trade Zone and defer the payment of duties until that merchandise is shipped out again. The creation of such zones offered the federal government a way to encourage imports and exports. For example, he said:

3M could import goods and materials for a given product from manufacturers all over the globe, ship them here to a Foreign Trade Zone and assemble them, using American workers, into a specific product. Duties are assessed only when that completed product is shipped out again to a buyer. And the duties paid on the finished product often are less than those that might have been assessed on the individual components, an arrangement that often eases a manufacturer's cash flow.

As a public warehouse site for Foreign Trade Zone 119, Murphy Warehouse was granted a license as a United States Customs Examination Station in 1991. During that process, the company also secured a Container Freight Station license. Finally, Customs asked the company to become a U.S. Customs General Order Facility for products which may be seized on occasion. Richard Murphy explained that,

> The containers are shipped in now by various trucking companies, although we still do some of this locally. When E. L. Murphy Trucking was operating, we hauled a lot of foreign trade containers, even though our own Foreign Trade Zone had not yet been established. The first year the Zone was in use here, we had thirty entries. Ten years later we were up to 300.

All of the company's international services are housed in a new entity he created: the Midwest International Logistics Center—MILC, for short—within the Murphy Industrial Park.

Another milestone loomed when the two elder Murphy brothers, Ed and Dick, realized it was time for a change in command. Ed Murphy had retired from Murphy Motor Freight, and at the Murphy Warehouse Companies, Dick Murphy had begun to turn the management reins over to Richard and Laurie Murphy. While Dick Murphy Sr., remained chairman, Richard Murphy was named president and chief executive officer of the Murphy Warehouse Company in 1993; Laurie Murphy had been named vice president in 1989. For a time the companies paused as the two men examined the issues surrounding buying each other out, and decided not to do so. As Richard Murphy described it:

> The company's growth really began again at that point. It was a huge decision for this company and its future because it moved us from short-term to long-term planning. Eventually it moved the warehouse from leasing space into ownership of real estate; it moved us out of our heavy orientation to the

food and grocery industry, which once was very recession-proof, but with deregulation, industry changes, and margin pressures, it had become so price-sensitive that it didn't make sense to stay heavily into it.

The Murphys, Dick and Richard, went after the paper, beverage, and electrical generating industries and they built warehouses specific to those industries. They began shipping electrical generators to China. As Richard Murphy, explained it:

> In the late 1980s and early 1990s we made a concerted effort to enter the paper industry, in particular paper rolls and flat stock. Our first major account was the Blandin Paper Company in Grand Rapids, Minnesota. For this we leased space in the Quebecor building in northeast Minneapolis. The paper business needed rail connections. We'd traditionally been on the Chicago Northwestern line, now owned by the Union Pacific, but Blandin used the Burlington Northern rails and we needed to be there too, in order to handle their business. Part of our strategy, which really picked up steam when we started with Blandin, was to be on all the major railroads that service the Twin Cities, and today we're on all of those major carriers.

The third and the fourth generation of Murphys: Laurie, Richard, and Dick.

Lack of enough rail dock doors at the Quebecor building, however, was hampering the Murphy company's growth. Then Murphy was asked to handle all the international shipping, mainly to China, for the Onan Company. Founded in Minneapolis in 1920, Onan builds electrical generators and industrial engines. It entered the international market in the 1930s, but during World War II the government's need to provide electricity to far flung fighting arenas positioned Onan for major postwar expansion. In China, in the 1980s, the government-owned power grid was suffering two or three brownouts a day, Richard Murphy explained, and its factories needed the backup power that Onan's generators could provide.

In 1994, with the Blandin and Onan needs outgrowing Quebecor space and more shipping capacity required on the Burlington Northern tracks, the Murphy company made another major decision: Build its own space. That was Northtown I in Fridley, a 265,700 square-foot warehouse with space for thirty trucks and ten indoor rail docks. The rail docks were a unique feature, admirably suited to the Minnesota climate. They allowed railroad cars to move indoors for loading and unloading. There were safety reasons for this, too, as Richard Murphy explained:

> It was much more efficient for our people to work indoors, especially during our long, cold winters. We got the approval from the railroad unions for this and also for what is called "close clearance." Normally, the distance between the dock and the railcar door is three feet. Ours is twelve inches. That's an ergonomic advantage too, because our guys can stand at the proper height to open the car doors.

In 1995 the Blandin paper business moved into Northtown I, but its continuing expansion set off a series of musical chairs. Around the same time, Onan also moved into Northtown I, then asked the Murphy company for more space to house both Onan's domestic operations and its distribution center. Leasing another 150,000 or so square feet to Onan left Murphy Warehouse with no space of its own in which to grow. A scant eighteen months later, the Murphy company put up Northtown II, also in Fridley. Both were built on land the Murphys bought from Burlington Northern. Onan moved into Northtown II, taking up all of its 194,000 square feet and clearing Northtown I for the Murphy company's own warehouse operation.

It was clear, however, that another major milestone, the construction of Northtown III, was not far off. Completed in November 1999, the facility actually was the product of a dream by several Onan offi-

'WE BECAME LEADERS IN SAFETY'

One of my father's lifelong business strategies concerned safety in the work place. Top priority always was given to holding monthly safety meetings and providing all employees with safe, properly working equipment to do their jobs. He took great pride in providing the safest work place possible. His philosophy was to stay ahead of work place injuries, and he led the industry in that approach. In 1975 he received the President's Safety Award from the Minnesota Trucking Association. E. L. Murphy Trucking Company and Murphy Warehouse received many yearly safety awards from ATA, MTA, and other national safety organizations.

With Paul Welna at the warehouse and Ron Gunderson and Gordy Keeler at the trucking company managing the safety programs, the Murphy companies had an excellent record. My father spoke often at the monthly safety meetings. (Few presidents had this hands-on concern.) He felt that keeping safety concerns in front of his employees would cut down on the number and severity of injuries. He always ended his speeches by reminding employes to work safely for themselves first, their families second, and the company third. He would add that if an employee did receive a serious injury, it was the employee who suffered the most, but the company suffered, too, in losing a valuable, well-trained worker.

In the late 1970s, Paul Welna helped create a progressive Return-to-Work program. In 1986 the company instituted a Back Injury Prevention Program, which was an innovative concept. Dr. Tom Votel of St. Paul had developed a back support safety belt for companies whose employees did a lot of heavy lifting. He suggested

that we hire Dave Thorson, a physical therapist, to train our men on proper lifting techniques. Dave ran a two-year series of Back Injury Prevention training sessions and still comes out each year to re-emphasize those concepts. Code 70, the task code for "warm-ups," was developed as part of this program. For more than fifteen years, we have paid our men to do ten minutes of warm-up and stretching exercises. All of these efforts have been effective in reducing on-the-job injuries and maintaining our reputation throughout the industry as leaders in safety issues.

In 2003, we received our OSHA/MnSharp certification. This ensures our OSHA compliance. We were the eleventh company in Minnesota to receive this honor.

Laurie Murphy

Dave Thorson (right) showing Dick Baker how to lift properly. Thorson is a registered physical therapist.

cials to establish their distribution center on their own property. In 1987 the Cummins Engine Company of Columbus, Indiana, had bought Onan and Cummins refused to allow the company to build on land Onan had owned because of the financial impact of fixed assets on shareholder value. After reaching out to the traditional real estate development community and finding no one able to meet their requirements, Onan turned to Murphy. Would Murphy buy the land from Onan and build the facility for them? This became Northtown III, but not before a serious problem was resolved. The property was not an ancient Indian burial ground, as Dick Murphy had encountered some thirty years earlier, but it had been an old pole-treating facility and it was polluted—a Superfund site. Most of the needed cleanup had been completed, Richard Murphy recalled, but another $1 million-worth of work remained.

> We had two conditions: that the site be brought to the point so that it was no longer listed as a Superfund site and that there would be no deed restrictions to preclude us from selling the site in the future. Both conditions were met and we went ahead with the project. We basically took a site with a negative worth of $400,000 and turned it into a facility that paid close to half a million in property taxes as of 2001.

Northtown III, a $13.4 million, 406,000 square-foot distribution center, opened in 1999. The city of Fridley and the state of Minnesota "were ecstatic" over the results, Richard Murphy said. Both had helped. The Metropolitan Council and the Minnesota Department of Trade and Economic Development had provided grants for some of the rest of the cleanup, and the city of Fridley had contributed funds to help with the extraordinary amount of site work needed at the Northtown III location. Regulations required on-site storm water retention ponds. To drain water from the site, pipes had to run from the ponds, underneath some railroad tracks, a county road, and a city park to a stream, a distance of half-a-mile. Richard Murphy described a unique aspect of the new building:

> There was a physical connection between the distribution center and the Onan plant—I call it an "on-grade skyway." Raw materials from the distribution center run along the skyway into the plant itself and the finished goods return the same way. It's a nice system. And it met the dreams of the Onan people by saving them more than three-quarters-of-a-million dollars in cartage costs.

PRAIRIE GRASSES AT MURPHY WAREHOUSES

Something new and certainly unique has been added to each of the three newer Murphy Warehouses in Fridley, Minnesota. Thirteen acres of prairie grasses have been planted as a reminder of the once-open land that surrounded this area.

"I wanted to create a new aesthetic for industrial properties, one that raised the bar on design quality," Richard T. Murphy Jr., ASLA, explained. This was borne out by the University of Minnesota's Design Center for the American Urban Landscape using Murphy's projects in illustrating an example of good industrial design. Drawing on his background in landscape architecture, Richard Murphy said, "I wanted a memorable look so people would associate a nice property with Murphy. I wanted us to be seen as a good neighbor within the neighborhood. The key was to frame the natural looking prairie with green lawn to give it the crisp, clean edge expected in today's residential neighborhoods."

There was a practical side as well. "Prairie grasses create an ecologically friendlier environment than the traditional lawn. They are less expensive to maintain because no sprinkler irrigation is required and no weekly lawn mowing or fertilizing are needed. Periodic maintenance is required during the summer in addition to the every 2-3 years burning to simulate the natural ecology of a prairie from lightening fires for regeneration and other positive impacts."

As part of this innovative approach to industrial landscaping, the plans for the prairie sites adjacent to each warehouse included planting a variety of trees that are typical of Minnesota's hardwood forests that once abutted this prairie ecology. The 657 trees that were planted at the three Murphy Warehouses represent the equivalent of having planted three trees at each of 219 single-family homes.

Then there is the Anheuser-Busch distribution center in Coon Rapids and "the little extra help" the company received in establishing it. Anheuser-Busch turned out to be another milestone. As Richard Murphy tells the story, the Murphys learned early in 1995, that the giant St. Louis brewing company was considering putting up a distribution center in the Twin Cities. It was to be Anheuser-Busch's second such center; its first was in Portland, Oregon.

> We first pursued the opportunity through our rail contracts. When that got nowhere, we went directly to Anheuser-Busch. We were at the bottom of their list because all other bidders were national organizations. We did a lot of hard work. We showed them a series of options. Anheuser-Busch didn't have any sites at that point, and hadn't even selected a railroad.

This was to be a heavily rail-oriented, in-bound facility, with Burlington Northern or Union Pacific as the major carriers, so Murphy showed the company sites on those lines. The following January, Richard Murphy walked brewing company representatives through Northtown I. "They immediately fell in love with the indoor rail

Murphy Rigging loads a vessel/tank on a tractor with dolly trailer, which is an extra-long permitted load.

facility and wanted it." Then, as he recalled it, nature, over which no one present that day had any control, stepped in with that "little extra help."

> What everyone still remembers to this day, especially the Anheuser-Busch people, was that it was 20 below zero and they'd never experienced anything like that in their entire lives. In that weather, when we were explaining the concept of the indoor rail, it looked good to them. That made a big impression.

A site in Coon Rapids finally was selected and a 154,000 square-foot warehouse opened there in September 1997. "We must have interviewed 500 people and hired twenty-three for that project, at a time when hiring was difficult," Laurie Murphy remembered. Peter Kronschnabel was selected to operate the new facility.

The warehouse was built to handle eighteen railcars indoors, but averages eighteen to twenty-four a day. "Anheuser-Busch tells us that we're the benchmark for all the other outside third-party distribution centers we have since opened," Richard Murphy noted. "To date there are seven of them, including Minneapolis and Portland."

> Ours was the model as to building design and how the contract was to be structured from a legal aspect. Anheuser-Busch since has built facilities in Detroit, Oklahoma City, Boston, St. Louis, and Waco, Texas. The numbers show that we're the best in productivity so far. We've held our costs to the point where, even five years later, we haven't needed to increase our bid costs. Each of the new buildings has been designed to be multifunctional. Each has been built with the intention that it could be sold if the economy sours. If we have to release them, we can do so.

As of 2004, a century after Edward L. Murphy bought two horses and a wagon, the company that grew out of that opening shot at entrepreneurship has survived depressions and deregulation. While the Murphy trucks no longer haul for the vanished E. L. Murphy Trucking Company or Murphy Motor Freight Lines, they still operate twenty trucks servicing customers in the local five-state area, moving

Paperless warehouse: computer terminal mounted on a forklift.

Murphy Family Officers:

RICHARD T. MURPHY SR.

Richard T. Murphy Sr., is the founder and present chairman of the Murphy Warehouse Company and Murphy Rigging. His background, training and education, along with a vast array of community involvements, have been centered in Minnesota.

He graduated from St. Thomas Military Academy in 1942 and was immediately inducted into the army where he served until 1944. After graduating from the University of Minnesota in 1946, he joined the family firm as secretary of E. L. Murphy Trucking Company; in 1947 he was named executive vice president, and in 1952 he became president. That year, also, he founded Murphy Warehouse Company and incorporated it in 1956 as a separate entity of the trucking company.

He has held many posts on the local and national level with organizations within the transportation industry. He has been president of Specialized Carriers & Riggers of America; American Warehouse Association; Allied Distribution; Associated Warehouses; Heavy Specialized Carriers of America; Local Cartage National

Conference; the Minneapolis Transfermen's Association; the St. Paul Transfermen's Association; and the Minnesota Trucking Association.

As a trustee, he has chaired the executive committee of St. Thomas Academy, and he has been a trustee of Mounds Park Hospital Foundation, and Sienna Heights College in Adrian Michigan.

He has been president and a director of the Ramsey County Historical Society and in 2003 was named director emeritus. He also has served on the Council of the Minnesota Historical Society and as its president. He has represented the Ramsey County Historical Society on the St. Paul Historical Preservation Commission, and has been the Commission's chairman. He has been a director of the Lake County (Minnesota) Historical Society, the Catholic Defense League of Minnesota, the Alliance for the Mentally Ill of Minnesota, and the Upper Midwest Museum of Transportation.

The many awards he has received for his years of community service have included the Charles W. Holman Aviation Achievement (1963); Fellow of the Michigan Academy of Science, Arts and Letters (1972); President-of-the-Year, Minnesota Motor Transport Association (1975); Distinguished Service Award, Archdiocese of St. Paul and Minneapolis (1979); Paul Harris Fellow Rotary International (1979); Hanes Alumni Honors Award, St. Thomas Academy, (1980); Golden Wheel Award for Distinguished Service, Specialized Carriers and Riggers Association (1981); Distinguished Service Award American Warehouse Association (1988); Lobaido Community Service Award from the Winter Carnival Association (1990); Catholic of the Year from the Catholic Defense League (1999); and the Preservation Alliance Lifetime Achievement Award for 2002. In 2002 Pope John Paul II named him a Knight of the Holy Sepulchre.

EDWARD L. MURPHY JR.

Edward Louis Murphy Jr., who is known to his friends as Ed and his family as Bud, graduated from Cretin High School in St. Paul, the University of Minnesota, and the University of Minnesota Law School. Following graduation, he joined the prestigious Minneapolis law firm of Stinchfield, Mackall & Crounse. Today that firm's successor, Mackall, Crounse & Moore, serves as the outside counsel for the Murphy Companies, just as its predecessor did beginning in the 1940s.

Ed Murphy left law school in 1936 to help his father start the E. L. Murphy Trucking Company. He subsequently returned to the University of Minnesota Law School and completed his degree. Following his father's heart attack in December 1941, Ed again left the practice of law to help manage the E. L. Murphy Trucking Company. In 1945, when Ed and his father brought Murphy Motor Freight Lines back into the Murphy fold, Ed served as president and later as

chief executive officer until his retirement in 1987.

While he was active as a business leader, Ed served for more than twenty years on the board of directors of the First National Bank (now US Bank), as well as on the boards of First Bank System, American Hoist and Derrick, J. L. Shiely Company, and the Waldorf Paper Company. He also served as a trustee of the University of St. Thomas in St. Paul.

In conjunction with his responsibilities as president and chief executive officer of Murphy Motor Freight Lines, Ed was actively involved in transportation industry organizations by serving as chair of the Regular Common Carriers Conference; vice chair of the American Trucking Association; president of the Middle West Motor Freight Bureau; president of Minnesota Motor Trucking Association; and board member of the Truckers Employers Association.

back and forth between the Murphy Industrial Park in southeast Minneapolis, the company's warehouse/distribution center facilities in the Northtown Park in Fridley, and the nine other warehouse centers the company operates.

The company that began life with two men, father and son, has, as of 2004, about 200 employees who handle freight from some 76,415 truckloads and between 9,000 and 10,000 rail cars that flow in and out of the warehouses each year.

Although Dick Murphy had begun to withdraw from active management of the company, and despite his long years with the trucking and warehouse industries, he had developed and maintained outside interests. One of them was the Civil Air Patrol (the CAP):

> After I came home from the army in 1944, a friend told me he needed someone to teach military courtesy and discipline to some young people at St. Thomas Academy. That's how I became involved with the Civil Air Patrol. I stayed with it and wound up as wing commander for the entire state. I was a

RICHARD T. MURPHY JR.

Richard T. Murphy Jr., succeeded his father as president and chief executive officer of the Murphy Warehouse Company in 1993 and Murphy Rigging and Erecting in 2000. After spending a semester studying in Japan while he was an undergraduate, he received the BLA and BED degrees in 1975 in Landscape Architecture and Environmental Design from the University of Minnesota's Institute of Technology. Richard subsequently earned an MLA from the Harvard Graduate School of Design, Cambridge, Massachusetts, in 1980 and an MBA in 1986 from the Carlson School of Management at the University of Minnesota. He was inducted into Sigma Lambda Alpha, the Landscape Architecture honor society in 1982 and in 1986 was elected to Beta Gamma Sigma, the management honor society.

He is chairman of the Executive Committee at the Center for Transportation Studies, University of Minnesota, and past chairman of the Minnesota Trucking Association. During the Minnesota Legislature's 2000-2001 session, he was one of three private industry representatives on the Commissioner of MNDOT's Ramp Meter Study.

He is a member of the Warehouse Education and Research Council (WERC) and the Council of Supply Chain Management Professionals (CSCMP; formerly known as the Council of Logistics Management), where he was a past Roundtable president. While serving as CSCMP's Roundtable chairperson, he directed sixty-two Roundtables in nine countries and as a member of the Education Strategies Committee completed a major project to provide marketing text authors and marketing course instructors with a "toolbox" of supply chain/logistics core knowledge information, cases, lecture notes, and chapter outlines. In 2005 he will chair CSCMP's General Conference, which will bring together more than 4,000 supply chain professionals. He has spoken often at WERC and CSCMP annual meetings on such subjects as "The Strategic Planning Process," "Outsourcing Non-Standard Services," and "Leadership."

He is on the board of the International Warehouse Logistics Association (IWLA) and during the past four years has been actively involved in the Workplace Ergonomics issue as a member of the OSHA Small Business Advisory Review Panel. He delivered testimony at the OSHA Ergonomics hearing in Washington, D. C., in 2000, the U.S. Department of Labor's Public Forum on Ergonomics in Chicago in 2001, and the Minnesota Department of Labor and Industry's Ergonomics Review Board in St. Paul in 2002.

He is a licensed Landscape Architect and a member of the American Society of Landscape Architects (starting in 1973). Since 1987 he has taught the Professional Practice course as Adjunct Professor of Landscape Architecture at the College of Architecture and Landscape Architecture, University of Minnesota. He has also held teaching positions at SUNY, Syracuse as well as the Harvard Graduate School of Design while a graduate student. His professional practice expertise is exercised whenever Murphy Warehouse Company develops new facilities.

colonel and I flew with the CAP. At first we had AT6s, which were Air Force training planes.

Dick Murphy's years at St. Thomas Academy and the military training offered there reinforced his interest in the military. He also

LAURIE MAY MURPHY

Laurie M. Murphy was the first of Dick Murphy's family to join the E. L. Murphy Trucking Company in 1982 as assistant in marketing. She was named purchasing manager the following year, and corporate secretary in 1984. In the meantime, she followed a family maxim that experience beyond the family business was important. In 1972, after graduating from the University of Minnesota with a degree in the Humanities and English, she joined B. Dalton Booksellers as assistant manager of its downtown Minneapolis store. A year later she became assistant store manager for B. Dalton's Southdale store, and subsequently moved to a position of assistant buyer for the store. Finally, between 1976 and 1982, she was buyer of bestsellers.

Putting the experience that she had gained at B. Dalton's to work for E. L. Murphy Trucking Company in 1982, Laurie was an assistant in marketing. She then moved in 1985 to the Murphy Warehouse Company where in 1989 she became vice president and secretary. Laurie subsequently earned an MBA (1989) from the Carlson School of Business at the University of Minnesota.

Laurie Murphy is a member of the St. Paul Rotary Club, the American Warehouse Association, Carlson Executive CEMBA, the Hibernian Society, the Minnesota Family Business Council, and Kappa Alpha Theta Sorority. Following the family tradition of giving back to the community, she has served two three-year terms on the board of directors of the Ramsey County Historical Society, including membership on the Society's Editorial Board, which supervises production of its books and its quarterly journal, Ramsey County History.

Involved as a volunteer in many areas, Laurie has shared her leadership skills and talents with many community organizations. Following service on the board of the Guild of Catholic Women, which focuses on mental health needs,

Laurie served as President of the Guild during its 100th Anniversary year. She has been Chair of the Catholic Committee on Scouting (Indianhead), Vice-chair of the Catholic Committee on Scouting (Twin Cities), Committee Chair of Nativity Troop #67 and has served in many other Cub Scouting and Boy Scouting board positions. Archbishop Harry Flynn of the Archdiocese of St. Paul and Minneapolis appointed Laurie to the executive board of the Archdiocese's Sesquicentennial Committee. She also served as Co-Chair of the Taste of the Archdiocese Festival and was elected secretary of the Minnesota Irish Fair.

In addition Laurie has been a long-term board member of the Cradle of Hope, the St. Thomas Mothers Club, the St. Thomas Auction Committee, the Corpus Christi Catechism Board, the Highland Central Hockey Banquet Committee, and the Nativity Council of Catholic Women. She has also chaired several committees for Nativity Home and School. Laurie served a three-year term on the first parish Council for Nativity Church and has been co-chair of many areas of the Nativity County Fair. In addition to serving six years as Director of the Sunday Morning Nursery Program at Nativity, Laurie has taught second grade in the Religious Education Program since 1997. A graduate of Derham Hall High School, Laurie enthusiastically raced sailboats for twelve years.

Utilizing her background in book publishing, she has helped produce five histories of the Twin Cities region, including this account of the history of the Murphy family and its companies. Her other book-length projects include the Minnetonka Yacht Club Centennial History *(Minnetonka Yacht Club, 1982);* Saint Paul–The First 150 Years *(The Saint Paul Foundation, 1991);* Jane Gibbs: "Little Bird That Was Caught" *(Ramsey County Historical Society, 1998);* and "You Shall Be My People," A History of the Archdiocese of Saint Paul and Minneapolis *(Editions du Signe, 1999).*

developed a love of history. It was an interest that has propelled him into the leadership of both the Ramsey County Historical Society and the Minnesota Historical Society. He has served each institutution as president and as a longtime board member. In 2003 the Ramsey County Historical Society named him director emeritus.

There have been other community interests, such as the St. Paul Rotary Club where he has been a member for more than fifty years— the club's oldest member in terms of service. "Dad steered me toward Rotary on the premise that that's where the more influential business and professional men belonged," Murphy remembered. "He said I should get in while I was young." He has followed in his father's foot- steps as a member of the Town and Country Club and the Minnesota Club. He and his wife Helen were co-chairmen in 2000 of the Com- mittee for the Celebration of the 150th Anniversary of the founding of the Archdiocese of St. Paul and Minneapolis. As part of the cele- bration, they commissioned sculptor Glenn Terry to create a statue of the apostle St. Paul as a gift to the archdiocese and the Cathedral of St. Paul in memory of Dick Murphy's mother, May, who had played the organ there.

With the expansion of Murphy Warehouse now in his hands and his father watching from some distance, Richard Murphy reflected on that relationship:

> I'm the fourth generation son to work for his father in this
> family business. One of the things I admire about my father

A Quality Certification

In July of 2003, Murphy Warehouse received its ISO 9001 Quality Certification. ISO 9001 is an international standards organization. The certi- fication means that all of Murphy's order fulfill- ment, purchasing, customer service and trans- portation processes and procedures are standard procedures and that we have a recognized, ac- cepted way of performing these tasks in the ware- house industry. In short, we do it right the first time and we do what we say we do.

ISO/Quality is a management system. We undertook this Quality Management System to verify our current procedures, to tighten up non- conforming areas, to continuously improve, and to enhance our working partnerships with our customers. We are the first warehouse company in the country to have the ISO system on com- puter. Most ISO/Quality systems are paper-based, with countless manuals, and have many updat- ing problems. Our computerized system means that the system is always alive and current. If a procedure is changed, it is changed instanta- neously for all users. A few of our customers al- ready have adopted ISO, but we believe it is the future and the way to go.

Laurie Murphy

is that he has been very good, as hard as it must have been for him, at giving up the authority and control as I continued to grow. Obviously, that left him with little to do in a business that was his life. He did it gracefully, but I know how difficult it was.

Richard Murphy himself is aware of the need for a challenging avocation. With his undergraduate degree in Landscape Architecture from the University of Minnesota, he has kept his fingers in the design field, teaching the professional practice course for the past eighteen years at the University's College of Architecture and Landscape Architecture. He believes he's learned much about management in the process. As for the future:

> I think the company's future is good. We need to keep our eyes open and stay with the trends. After the dot.com debacle, people realized that products are still products and they still have to be moved. As much as everybody would like to get away from inventory because of the costs of handling it, that's tough to do. Because we are the Hertz (#1) in our market, we have to be careful and always think and act like Avis (#2 "We try harder"). That is our challenge.

Another warehouse or two might lie in the future. As for the international market, it might expand for the Murphys.

> We sit in the middle of North America. That's how we see ourselves, not as Upper Midwest Minnesota. The major rail connections from the Asian market come through here from Portland and Seattle on the Burlington Northern.

He has a strong sense of the importance of the people who work for the Murphy Companies. It's a sense Laurie Murphy shares.

In Richard Murphy's words, "To compete and survive, we want to become a preferred employer within our industry. We've come a long way from the days when my great grandfather could post a notice ordering all teamsters to report for work on Sundays to care for the horses, and 'if any driver in our employment is not satisfied with this rule, he can quit.' We want to be an employee-friendly organization for our employees. Our people are what make us what we are. As much as high tech is infiltrating industry, it's not going to replace the flexibility that comes with working through people rather than technology."

One of Murphy Warehouse's new buildings showing the prairie grasses.

Appendix 1

The Evolution of a Warehouse

Dick Murphy Sr., pointing to a new warehouse building in Fridley. It was constructed in 1993 on a Burlington Northern railroad yard.

Richard Jr., Dick, and Laurie Murphy signing a beam that will be visible from the floor of a new warehouse.

The frame of the warehouse goes up.

Next, the roof panels go up.

"Tilt up" panels installed.

The cement flood is poured.

The first railcar is delivered. A pizza party with balloons and a green ribbon is held for employees.

The first railcar is unloaded. Here are Bob Doerr, Leroy Ives (back turned to camera), Frank Cullinan, Richard Murphy Jr. (partially obscured), Ted Sheffield, and an unidentified Burlington Northern employee.

Paul Welna and Dick Murphy Sr. "Let's build another one!"
And they did.

Murphy Warehouse Company
Murphy-Owned Facilities Data

	Northtown I Fridley, Minn. (built 1994)	Northtown II Fridley, Minn. (built 1996)	Northtown III Fridley, Minn. (built 1999)	Main Minneapolis, Minn. (built 1902–1978)
Site Area	15.5 acres	11.37 acres	26.1 acres	21.39 acres
Building Size	265,735 sq. ft.	194,500 sq. ft.	406,164 sq. ft.	650,000 sq. ft.
Prairie Size	3.5 acres	2.5 acres	7.0 acres	0 acres
Trees Planted	199	115	343	88
Ceiling Clear Height	26 to 32.5 ft.	30 ft.	30 ft.	18 to 20 ft.
Typical Bay Spacing	40 ft x 40 ft.	40 ft. x 40.67 ft.	40 ft. x 40 ft.	35 ft. x 35 ft.
Trailer Docks	29	23	55	75
Trailer Parking Spaces	30	30	70	55
Rail Docks	10 indoor	3–4 indoor	6 indoor + 3 exterior	7 exterior
Rail Service	BNSF	BNSF	MN Common (CP, CN, UP, BNSF)	UP

Abbreviations

BNSF	Burlington Northern Santa Fe
CP	Canadian Pacific
CN	Chicago Northwestern
UP	Union Pacific

Appendix 2

Trucks, Tractors, and Trailers

WHO WERE THE DRIVERS AND WHERE WERE THEY GOING?
CAN YOU GUESS?

Rubber-tired Murphy Transfer and Storage truck moving a Lake Minnetonka boat, probably in the 1920s.

Hauling an old fire wagon pumper on a single-drop trailer in the early 1980s.

Three turbine parts on a tridem lowbed heading for the Westinghouse Company, Charlotte, N. C.

A boiler on a custom-built Cozad trailer for Northwest Copper in Oregon.

A double-drop trailer hauling for Lull Engineering in the early 1980s.

A tank on a double-drop trailer,
E. L. Murphy Trucking, early 1980s.

Auger on a flatbed, early 1980s, E. L. Murphy Trucking.

Transformers heading to General Electric on a tandem flatbed.

General Electric engine on removable gooseneck trailer.

Fiberglass sheets on a trailer. Which trailer? Readers?

A new Cozad tractor-trailer in the
early 1980s.

An engine for a Pan American jet airplane, September, 1977.

E. L. Murphy Trucking Company loading air freight in the 1980s.

Art Cromey's new Cozad trailer,
November, 1984.

A military tank on a removable
gooseneck trailer.

A tilt-a-bed trailer with an O ring on board. Used by E. L. Murphy Trucking Company, in the 1980s, and still in use today by Murphy Rigging.

A pressure vessel on a Cozad trailer with nine axles, late 1970s.

And now for the mystery picture. Are these snowplows on a flatbed? Snowmobiles? Readers?

E. L. Murphy Trucking hauling bridge sections in the 1960s.

Powerline tops for a transformer being hauled by E. L. Murphy Trucking Company in the early 1980s.

Appendix 3

Rigging, Erecting, and Relocating

Tom Dibble and John Liggett directing the loading of an MRI machine around 1985.

June 29, 2004, Murphy Rigging moves restored New York Eagle sculpture to Overlook Park on Summit Avenue. Mrs. Richard T. Murphy Sr., coordinated the move.

The Versa Lift with extended counterweight. It's moving a machining center at the Machinery Show in the Minneapolis Convention Center, in 1999. Tim Lyons is on the far left with Rodney Erickson, and Bob Liggett.

Rodney Erickson, far right, and John Liggett guiding a transformer move in 1999.

A 90,000-pound fermentation tank being hoisted up and put in to a plant via the roof. Rigging had to remove the old tank and rebuild the catwalk around the new tank. Left to right are John Olson, Rodney Erickson, Mike Bennett, Marty Jarmko, Darren Julin and two unidentified customers who are kneeling.

Murphy Rigging moved this sculpture of the apostle St. Paul to the Cathedral of St. Paul in 2000. The sculpture was commissioned by Dick and Helen Murphy in honor of Dick Murphy's mother, May McGinnis Murphy, who once played the organ at the Cathedral.

A sad day for Murphy Rigging as staff members attend the funeral for coworker Rodney Erickson. Front row, left to right, Tim Lyons, Bob Liggett, and Gary Grohoski; second row, left to right, John Olson, Tom Dibble, John Liggett (partially hidden), John Martin, and Glen Holmes; third row, left to right, Mike Bennett, Darren Julin, Chad Pomeroy, Robert Matzke, and Craig Hinschberger; fourth row, left to right, Bill Reller, Jeff LaBerge, and Brad Sass.

Pat Sullivan and her husband, George. Pat ran the Murphy Rigging office for thirty years.

The gantry system lifting an injection molding machine. The machine went up over the plant's roof before it could be lowered into the building.

Appendix 4

Boxes, Bags, and Rolls

A Murphy Warehouse fleet of forklifts in the mid-1970s

Ted Sheffield unloading pallets
in one of the new
Murphy warehouses.

A Great Way To Get Loaded

No matter how or where you've been shipping in the Upper Midwest and Montana, your first taste of our LTL FREIGHT CONSOLIDATION COST SAVINGS will sweeten your pallet.

Come on — let's get loaded. Call or write today for your Distribution Cost Analysis packet.

WAREHOUSE COMPANY

701 24th Avenue S.E., Minneapolis, MN 55414 ● Call Bob Eginton at: 612-623-1200

Bob Eginton, vice president of sales, posing with this award-winning ad from the early 1980s.
Bob has passed away and is missed by his Murphy friends.

A warehouse worker filling an order.

*Bob Baker, left, going over
the Preventative Maintenance
checklist with Doug Horn,
vice president for
business development.*

Frank Cullinan using a squeeze clamp to unload paper at one of the Murphys' new warehouses in 1996.

Head mechanic Bob Baker seated in a tractor while Wayne Raiche, head of building maintenance, inspects one of the new Mack tractors.

Julie Nepine demonstrating the two-way radio system with which each forklift is equipped. With the system, the operations department can contact any forklift driver in the warehouse.

Appendix 5

Key Business Events for the Murphy Companies, 1972–2004

DATE	EVENT
3/27/1972	"Local Cartage Permit" granted by the Minnesota Public Service Commission.
Summer 1978	Building 38 ("The Triangle") constructed at the 701 Minneapolis warehouse. Building 38 ties all buildings at the site together and provides indoor truck docks for increased security.
4/10/1979	"Irregular Route Common Carrier Authority" granted by the Minnesota Public Service Commission.
9/26/1979	"Freight Broker Authority" granted by the Interstate Commerce Commission.
1979	Paul Welna begins the Return to Work (RTW) Program.
2/9/1981	"Common Carrier Authority" granted by the Interstate Commerce Commission.
1/26/1982	"Courier Service Carrier Authority" granted by the Minnesota Public Utilities Commission.
6/1/1982	Laurie Murphy begins her first official day as a full-time associate of the E. L. Murphy Trucking Company.
2/1/1983	Murphy Company begins first major contract operation in the company's recent history by operating a facility for Sandoz Nutrition (now Novartis) in Minnetonka, Minn.

9/12/1983	Richard T. Murphy Jr. begins his first official day as a full-time associate of the E. L. Murphy Trucking Company.
4/1/1986	Dr. Tom Votel and Dave Thorson, RPT, begin the Back Injury Prevention Program at the Murphy Companies. This program is still in operation.
11/12/1987	"Container Freight Station (CFS) Authority" granted by the U.S. Customs Agency of the Department of the Treasury.
4/15/1991	"Customs Examination Station (CES) Authority" granted by the U.S. Customs Agency, Department of the Treasury.
2/19/1993	Lunch meeting with Bruce Opp of the Burlington Northern (BN) Railroad takes place to consider the availability of rail-owned property for sale to Murphy for construction of a new warehouse.
6/14/1993	A meeting with John Pope, AIA, of Pope Associates is held to discuss the design of a new warehouse.
7/1/1993	Murphy leases space in a Quebecor warehouse and starts its big growth effort in paper storage.
10/20/1993	Due to the rising cost of leasing warehouse space, the Murphy Board of Directors begins discussion of building a new warehouse.
1/1/1994	A meeting is held with Bill Reiling of Towle Inc. regarding the feasibility of building a new warehouse and questions relating to location and other factors.
1/18/1994	Another meeting is held with Bruce Opp of BN regarding the railroad's interest in working with the Murphy Companies.
2/22/1994	The Murphy Board of Directors discusses new construction feasibility and its financial ramifications.
2/25/1994	The Murphy Board of Directors meets with Bill Towle to review warehouse concepts and feasibility of building a new warehouse in Fridley.
2/28/1994	Interview with Ryan Companies.

3/10/1994   Another meeting with Bruce Opp of BN regarding Fridley land availability and its cost.

3/17/1994   Interview of Opus (Pat Dady).

3/18/1994   Interview of KA plus Pope Associates and Westwood Planning.

4/25/1994   Meeting with representatives of Onan Company (Woody Nelson) and Opus (Dave Bangasser) regarding a warehouse for Onan.

7/25/1994   First meeting with MIMLIC along with Mark Vanelli of Towle.

8/16/1994   Murphy purchases land from BN Railroad in Fridley for construction of a new warehouse.

8/22/1994   Opus begins construction of Northtown I warehouse.

9/15/1994   Closing takes place on warehouse project financing with First Bank (construction loan) and with MIMLIC (pre-Permanent Mortgage Commitment).

2/1/1995   Closing takes place on Permanent Mortgage Financing with MIMLIC for Northtown I warehouse.

2/8/1995   First BN train switches to rail siding that gives access to Northtown I's indoor docks.

7/11/1995   Certificate of Occupancy issued for Northtown I.

11/1/1995   Anheuser-Busch Brewing Company sends Murphy Companies an official bid package for the Minneapolis Distribution Center project.

1/31/1996   Representatives of Anheuser-Busch make their first tour of sites in Fridley, Brooklyn Park, Shakopee, Minneapolis, and Maple Grove for a proposed new Murphy warehouse. The temperature that day is -20° F, with a slight wind chill.

4/12/1996   A "Panel Placement Ceremony" takes place at Northtown II.

6/21/1996   A Certificate of Occupancy is issued for Northtown II.

7/22/1996	Closing takes place on Permanent Mortgage Financing with MIMLIC for Northtown II warehouse.
10/2/1996	Representatives of Anheuser-Busch and Murphy sign a contract for Northtown II warehousing at the Mackall Crouse office.
3/25/1997	Joseph Sellinger, Vice President for Operations at Anheuser-Busch signs Murphy contract.
3/27/1997	The first formal meeting for a new Cummins/Onan Distribution Center in Fridley is held. The land for the new warehouse is to be purchased from Onan.
9/13/1997	Construction of the Anheuser-Busch facility is completed.
9/15/1997	First inbound shipment of Anheuser-Busch product arrives at Northtown II.
9/28/1997	First outbound shipment of Anheuser-Busch product is shipped from Northtown II.
7/17/1998	Cummins/Onan Corporation starts moving products into Northtown II under a three-year lease.
9/4/1998	A major meeting with Cummins/Onan approves the concept of building Northtown III.
3/2/1999	Cummins Power Generation/Onan signs a "Third party and Sublease Agreement with Murphy. The agreement has a ten-year base with an option for an additional eleven years. The signing ceremony is held at Northtown II, which Onan was then leasing for its warehousing operations.
5/11/1999	A closing is held for Murphy to purchase Onan land for Northtown III.
7/28/1999	A "Panel Placement Ceremony" is held for the construction of the new Cummins/Onan warehouse at Northtown III.
11/5/1999	A Certificate of Occupancy is issued for the Onan building (Northtown III).

3/9/2000	Murphy's Northtown III warehouse wins City-Business' "Best in Real Estate Award" in the "New Industrial Development" category.
5/25/2000	The final mortgage closing on Northtown III takes place with TCF.
4/1/2001	Heart defibrillator devices are installed in all Murphy facilities as part of the company's safety program.
9/18/2001	A "Moment of Silence" is held throughout all Murphy facilities to honor those who died in the events of 9/11/2001 and their families.
7/21/2003	ISO 9001:2000 Certification awarded to Murphy Warehouse Company at its main facility. Murphy is the first warehouse to have Total Quality Management System (TQMS)'s computerized Quality System.
12/10/2003	ISO 9001:2000 Certification officially awarded to Northtown I, II, and III warehouses.
8/6/2003	Minnesota OSHA informs Murphy Companies that it will be recommended for MnSHARP Certification. With this certification, Murphy becomes the 11th company in Minnesota to achieve this OSHA status.
10/10/2004	Murphy Companies celebrate 100 years of continuous business operations under the management of the members of a single family.

Appendix 6

Murphy Family Tree

John Murphy* & Mary O'Brien*
    Jack Murphy*

Edward L. Murphy* & Ellen Brown*
    Ella Murphy* & Ibar Spellacy*
    Lillian Murphy* & Patrick Connolly, Sr.*

Edward Murphy Sr.* & Frances Tenner*
Edward Murphy Sr.* & May McGinnis*
    | Genevieve Murphy* & William G. Maas* |
        Karen Althea Maas & Preston Michael (Mickey) Smith
        Peter Maas & Margot Jena
            Katja Maas & James O'Brien
            Alexia Maas & Trond Henrikson
                Kayla Maas
                Jesse Maas

    | Edward L. Murphy Jr. & Mercedes Shiely |
        Edward L. (Mike) Murphy III & Mary Lynn Nelson
            Ryan Murphy
            Mary Murphy
        Shawne Murphy & Michael Monahan
            Meghan Monahan & Brian Brown
            Michael Monahan Jr.
            Liam Monahan
        Tara Murphy & Rick Varco
            Rick Varco
            Lynn Varco
            Glin Varco
            Cavan Varco
        Brenna Murphy & Austin Ditzler
        Megan Murphy & Doug Carnival
            Jenny Murphy Carnival
            Leighlin Murphy Carnival
        Kevin Shiely Murphy & Colleen Fitzpatrick
            Conor Murphy
            Padraic Murphy
        Brian Murphy & Jan Martland
            Patrick Murphy
            Nicholas Murphy

*deceased

▬▬▬ 1st Generation
▬▬▬ 2nd Generation
▭▭▭ 3rd Generation

192

Edward Murphy Sr. & May McGinnis (continued)

Dorothie Murphy & A. Gray Fellows*

Althea Murphy & James L. Nelson Sr.*
 Lynn Nelson & Richard Bisanz
  Ben Bisanz
  Sam Bisanz
  Alex Bisanz
 James L. Nelson Jr. & Debi Orff
  Amy Nelson
  Ashley Nelson
  James L. Nelson III

Richard Tenner Murphy Sr. & Helen Duffy
 Laurel May Murphy & Gordon Gill Bowers Jr.
  Gordon Gill Bowers III
 Richard Tenner Murphy Jr. & Kay Motteberg
  Alexandra Murphy
  Tenner McGinnis Murphy
  Libby Frances Murphy
  Madigan Murphy
 Patrick Duffy Murphy
 Sharon Murphy & David Garber
  Joshua Garber
  Benjamin Garber
  Thomas Murphy Garber
 Maureen Murphy & Harry Aro
  Bailey Murphy Aro

Mary Carole Murphy & Richard Faricy
 Althea Faricy
 Bridget Faricy & Phil Mykland

Patricia Murphy & George Benz Millard
 Ben Millard & Kathleen Sladek
  Collette Millard
 David Millard & Chieko Nagocka
  Mika Millard
  Kyoka May Millard
 Stephan Millard
 Megan Murphy Millard

Index

100 YEARS
MURPHY
WAREHOUSE COMPANY
RIGGING AND ERECTING

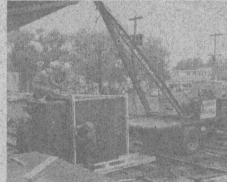